IRAN

IRAN

BY CHERESE CARTLIDGE

LUCENT BOOKS
SAN DIEGO, CALIFORNIA

THOMSON
GALE

Detroit • New York • San Diego • San Francisco
Boston • New Haven, Conn. • Waterville, Maine
London • Munich

Library of Congress Cataloging-in-Publication Data

Cartlidge, Cherese.
    Iran / by Cherese Cartlidge.
       p. cm. — (Modern nations of the world)
    Includes bibliographical references and index.
    Summary: Discusses the development of Iran from prehistoric times,
its geography, governments, religious beliefs, culture, social changes, and
modern problems.

    ISBN 1-56006-971-6 (lib.bdg. : alk. paper)

    1. Iran—Juvenile literature. [1. Iran.] I. Title.   II. Series.
    DS254.75 .C37 2002
  955—dc21

                                          2001005696

Copyright © 2002 by Lucent Books,
an imprint of The Gale Group
10911 Technology Place, San Diego, CA 92127
Printed in the U.S.A.

CONTENTS

INTRODUCTION

A NATION OF CONTRASTS

Iran is a nation of contrasts. Its climate includes frigid winters and boiling summers. The topography ranges from lofty mountains to deep valleys and from barren deserts to lush marshlands. And though it is known for its friendly, welcoming people, many of them highly educated and deeply religious, Iran also has a history of harshness—and by some standards barbarity—on the part of its leaders. Since the late 1970s, Iranian leaders have routinely denounced the United States, but Americans who have visited Iran almost uniformly report warm hospitality and a sincere desire to improve relations on the part of ordinary Iranians, who make a sharp distinction between the U.S. government and individual Americans.

Iranians make a similar distinction regarding their own government. The Islamic Republic of Iran has imposed restrictions on public behavior according to its interpretation of Islamic law: Gambling, alcohol, and drugs are forbidden, and women must be covered from head to toe when outside their homes. Iranians must conform to these restrictions, regardless of their true feelings. When they are not subject to restrictions, however, they make the most of the opportunity. Ana Briongos, a Spanish journalist who has traveled and studied in Iran periodically since the 1970s, writes about her experiences during a flight to Iran in March 1994:

> On the plane, an Air France flight from Paris, almost all of the passengers were Iranians; there can't have been more than six or seven foreigners. . . . Only half the women had their hair covered with scarves [as required by the Iranian dress code]. The men were much more lively and garrulous than the women: smiling and waving their hands about, continuously cracking jokes, laughing and telling stories as they walked up and down the aisle. . . . During the flight some of them ordered whisky, and others drank wine with their meal. [Alcohol

Iranian women dressed in the required cloak and headdress. The government in Iran restricts public behavior according to its interpretation of Islamic law.

is forbidden under Iranian law.] . . . As we passed over Tabriz, the first major city in Iran after crossing the border with Turkey, the air hostess announced that alcoholic beverages would no longer be served, and instructed passengers to hand in any alcohol they might have left, as well as empty bottles and lids. Every trace had to be eliminated.

One by one the women who had been travelling bareheaded covered themselves, and on arrival in Tehran, all of us, without exception, had our overgarments on and our headscarves in place. Even the French air hostesses.[1]

An Iranian family takes an outing in a rowboat.

The contradictions within Iran show up dramatically in the nation's governance. Iranians have repeatedly shown a desire for greater civil liberties and better international relations. For example, in national elections in 1997 and 2001, Iranians overwhelmingly voted for candidates who pledged to loosen restrictions on personal behavior and improve relations with other countries. These reforms, however, have been blocked by Iran's supreme leader, Ayatollah Khamenei, and the Council of Guardians, a government panel that reviews laws passed by the legislature and is dominated by conservative clerics.

The political and social situation in Iran is astoundingly complex. Yet Iran's status as a major source of the world's petroleum and as a potent regional military power make understanding this fascinating nation vital.

The Land and People of Iran

Iran has a total land area of 636,000 square miles, making it the second largest nation in the Middle East in terms of physical size. It shares a border with seven other nations, and its location in the midst of so many countries, along with its variable climate and diverse geography, has affected the character of Iranian society and culture.

The Peoples of Iran

Iranians are a diverse people. They come from a variety of regions and tribes, and various ethnic minorities make up about half of Iran's population of 66 million. According to author Robin Wright,

> Ethnically, Iranians reflect the geographic crossroads of Iran. . . . Iranians are Turkoman farmers and horse traders in the northeast, western Kurds, Baluchis (or "wanderers") who straddle the arid and unruly southeast border with Pakistan, Arabs on the southern coast, mountainous Lors (an Arab-Persian mix), nomadic herding tribes in the south and, in the cities, an array of Armenians, Mongols, Afghans and Indians—plus, of course, the majority Persians, who are everywhere, and the Turkish-speaking Azeris from the northernmost province of Azerbaijan, who account for up to a quarter of the population, making them the largest minority.[2]

Iran's large Azeri population lives mostly in three northwestern provinces, sandwiched between Turkey, Armenia, and the republic of Azerbaijan. Like other minority groups, many Iranian Azeris have close cultural and linguistic ties to ethnic Azeris in nearby countries.

Despite the nation's ethnic diversity, Iranians strive to unite their various ethnic groups. Supreme Leader Ayatollah Ali Khamenei, who is himself Azeri, said in a speech in 2000, "Let me express one sentence to you in your own sweet language [Azeri]. The Turk and the non-Turk peoples of Iran are all brothers, Muslims and devoted to the Islamic system in Iran."[3]

IRAN AT THE CROSSROADS

Iran is bordered on the north by Armenia, Azerbaijan, the Caspian Sea, and Turkmenistan; on the east by Afghanistan

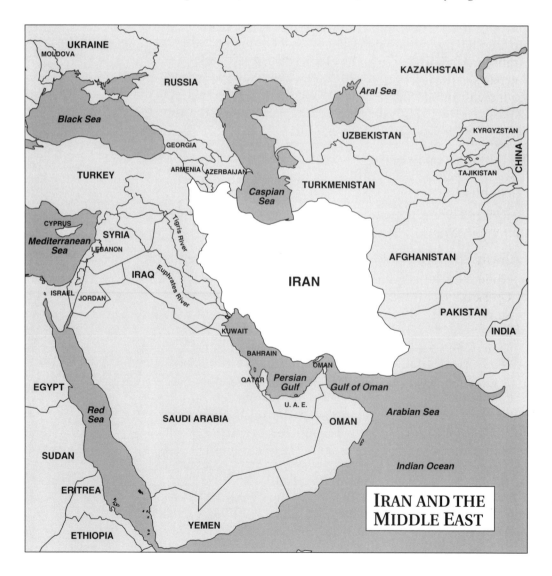

IRAN AND THE MIDDLE EAST

and Pakistan; on the west by Iraq and Turkey; and on the south by the Gulf of Oman and the Persian Gulf. Just across the Persian Gulf from Iran lie Bahrain, Kuwait, Qatar, Saudi Arabia, the United Arab Emirates, and Oman. Despite Iran's central location, it has been offset to some extent by the land's physical features. Most of Iran's borders are defined by mountain ranges and bodies of water.

Iranians today retain strong ties to the Persian culture that began to develop thousands of years ago. The culture's distinctiveness is due to the fact that, despite the country's physical isolation, Iran has been invaded many times in the past twenty-five hundred years by peoples who left their influence on the country, most notably the Greeks and the Arabs. Iranians often adapted to the foreign invaders, adopting parts of the foreign culture that seemed compatible with their own—but only up to a point. Author Christiane Bird observes,

> As a land bridge between the East and the West, Iran has been invaded countless times, . . . and yet has never succumbed completely to its conquerors. Instead, the country has coped with invasions by assimilating and adapting those aspects of the conquering cultures that it admired, such as Greek science and Chinese art, and leaving behind the rest. Says a Persian maxim: "Iranians are like wheat fields. When the storm comes, they bend; when the storm passes, they stand up again." Wrote the Greek historian Herodotus: "There is no nation which so readily adopts foreign customs as the Persians. As soon as they hear of any luxury they instantly make it their own."[4]

IRAN'S MOUNTAIN RANGES

The rugged terrain along much of Iran's border extends well into the nation's interior, making it one of the most mountainous countries in the world. Iran is dominated by two major mountain ranges that cover more than half its area. The Zagros Mountains in the west stretch more than one thousand miles from the northwest to the southeast, covering all of western Iran except the Khuzestan coastal plain on the Persian Gulf. Many of the peaks in the Zagros Mountains exceed ten thousand feet; the highest is Zard Kuh at nearly

THE SHAPE-SHIFTING ELBURZ MOUNTAINS

The Elburz, or Alborz, Mountains in northern Iran contain some of the highest peaks in the country. These lofty mountains seemed to Christiane Bird, an American who visited Iran in the late 1990s, to be alive and ever-changing. She describes her impression of these mountains in her book *Neither East nor West*.

> North Tehran backs up into the embrace of the Alborz Mountains, the most defining physical characteristic of the city. Bone dry and nearly devoid of vegetation in many parts, the Alborz are a living, breathing, shape-shifting presence that seems to stretch, yawn, buckle, and bend as it looms over the metropolis like a giant elephant in repose. One unexpected jerk in the middle of its usually protective sleep and it could kick the entire city right out of its foothills.
>
> Sometimes the Alborz—as high as the American Rockies—are all ridges, valleys, rocks, and sand, with sunlight illuminating a hidden cliff here, an unexpected rockslide there. Sometimes the Alborz are a flat, impenetrable, dun-colored wall, separating Tehran—and by extension, it seems, all of Iran—from the rest of the world. Sometimes the Alborz are sensual, red-hued, and comforting. Sometimes the Alborz are craggy, black, and forbidding.
>
> Sensitive to every nuance of light and atmosphere, the Alborz subtly change color with the day. Though often a dull

fifteen thousand feet. The Zagros range is up to two hundred miles wide and so rugged that road construction is difficult. As a result, the valleys between the mountains are isolated and are sparsely populated. Most of those who live in the area are pastoral nomads who exist by herding sheep and other domesticated animals.

The Elburz mountain range in the north runs along the southern coast of the Caspian Sea, from the border of Azerbaijan in the west toward Turkmenistan and Afghanistan. The volcanic Elburz range is narrower than the Zagros but higher. The highest peak, located at the center of the range, is Mount Damavand. This permanently snow-covered peak reaches 18,934 feet high. Mount Damavand is not only the

gray or maroon at first glance, closer looks reveal shifting green streaks, pink splotches, and purple peaks. A cloud passes over, casting down a blue patch.

The peaks of northern Iran's Elburz Mountains tower over Iran's countryside.

highest peak in the Elburz, but the highest mountain in Iran.

Low mountain ridges known as the eastern highlands rim Iran's eastern border, and, combined with the Zagros and Elburz ranges, they form a mountainous ring just inside Iran's boundaries. Despite its mountainous terrain, Iran has many areas suited to agriculture. In the north, a fertile but narrow strip of lowland, ranging from ten to twenty-five miles wide, lies between the Caspian Sea and the Elburz Mountains. Another coastal plain stretches along the coast of the Persian Gulf and the Gulf of Oman in the south. Crops such as wheat, rice, and barley are grown in these fertile coastal regions.

Mount Damavand, standing 18,934 feet high, looms above the Elburz range and is Iran's highest peak.

IRAN'S EARTHQUAKES

Iran's massive mountain ranges are active earthquake zones. The most vulnerable zone is in the northwest, where earthquakes leveled the city of Tabriz twice during the eighteenth century. In the last two decades of the twentieth century, there were approximately one thousand registered earthquakes in northwestern Iran. The worst of these occurred in 1990, in the fault zone where the Elburz and Zagros mountain ranges intersect. The earthquake registered 7.7 on the Richter scale and claimed the lives of forty-five thousand people.

Seismologists warn that Iran should expect major earthquakes about every five years. In 1997, the area around Ardabil in northwestern Iran was devastated by a quake that measured 7.1 and claimed the lives of more than 550 people. The frequency of serious earthquakes in the area puts the approximately 12 million people in the sprawling urban center of Tehran, many of whom live in poorly built high-rise apartments, in an extremely vulnerable position. Experts believe that if a major earthquake were to strike the city, it could mean the loss of thousands or perhaps millions of lives.

THE IRANIAN PLATEAU

Within the ring of mountains that surrounds much of Iran is a series of basins and plateaus collectively referred to as the Iranian Plateau. It was in the Iranian Plateau that Persian culture first began to flourish twenty-five hundred years ago, and it is here that the majority of Iranians live today.

The Iranian Plateau is a desert region consisting of sand, compacted silt, and rock. The plateau gradually merges into the Zagros and Elburz mountains. Iran's chief agricultural and urban areas are located in the foothills of these mountains, where the soil is fertile and runoff from mountain snow provides water. Tehran, the capital and largest city, is

Residents of this Iranian village grieve the loss of their home to an earthquake that claimed the lives of over 550 people in 1997.

A town on the edge of the Iranian Plateau. The majority of Iranians live in the urban and agricultural centers located in this fertile region.

located in the foothills of the Elburz, and Esfahan, a center for Persian culture and the nation's second largest city, is located in the foothills of the Zagros.

The Iranian Plateau contains two large deserts known as the Dasht-e-Lut and the Dasht-e-Kavir. These vast deserts lie in the northeastern and eastern areas of the plateau, stretching from Tehran in the northwest for a distance of about four hundred miles. These deserts are unsuitable for agriculture, so they remain largely uninhabited. One exception is Kerman, a rapidly growing oasis town in southeastern Iran. Kerman draws its water supply from *qanats*, underground water channels built many centuries ago.

IRAN'S WATERWAYS

Iran's underground water supplies, springs, rivers, and lakes have been important factors in the development of towns, cities, and agriculture. Although most of Iran's numerous rivers are too shallow for navigation and tend to dry up in the summer, since ancient times the rivers have supplied the water Iranians use to irrigate their crops. Iranians also depend on natural underground sources to supply water.

Iran's need for water is also served by reservoirs created by damming some rivers. For example, the Amir Kabir dam on the Karaj River creates a supply of drinking water for the sprawling metropolis of Tehran and provides hydroelectric power as well. Several other dams in Iran supply water for irrigation as well as for domestic use and hydroelectric power. In addition, the lakes formed by Iran's dams are also popular places for sailing and waterskiing.

Most of Iran's rivers drain into the Persian Gulf or the Caspian Sea, but a few empty into salty lakes in the interior basins. The largest of these is Lake Orumiyeh in northwestern Iran. Orumiyeh is a vast saline lake covering over two thousand square miles. Orumiyeh is much saltier than the ocean and so cannot support fish. As a result, its shores remain barren and undeveloped. Areas near the Caspian Sea, however, are more populous. The Caspian Sea has a lower salt content than Lake Orumiyeh and supports fish such as

A bridge spans one of Iran's numerous rivers. Iran depends on rivers, lakes, and streams, as well as underground sources, to provide water for domestic and agricultural use.

THE *QANAT*

In an arid country such as Iran, the ability to harness water is crucial for survival. An ancient method of irrigating the land and getting water to towns and villages, which is still in use in some areas, is the *qanat*—a system of wells and underground water channels. This system was first used on the Iranian Plateau more than twenty-five hundred years ago. In her book *The Iranians*, Sandra Mackey explains the importance of the *qanat* in Iran.

> During the sixth century B.C., the Persians, along with other societies on the Iranian plateau, assumed more complex forms as they made the transition from nomadism to settlement. Hostage to climate and topography, people could survive only by harnessing the great force that sustains life—water. Water meant hydration and food. It meant trees capable of providing shelter from the blaze of the sun and the desert. But rainfall in Iran averages only twelve inches a year. Cities and settlements stay alive with the melting snow running off the major mountain ranges that flows through [*joobs*], or concrete conduits, that border streets like narrow canals. Yet it is the *qanats* that testify in stark, visual terms to the Iranians' constant quest for water. Seen from the air, these miles of gently sloping underground tunnels intersected by well shafts that resemble giant mole holes lie on the landscape like ribbons. As old as Iran itself, the *qanats* bequeath or deny fertility to the land. The ancient Persians, recognizing the crucial link between water and life, summoned their first system of government to equitably distribute the precious, sparse resource.

sturgeon, salmon, perch, and pike. The Persian Gulf, which includes the Strait of Hormuz and the Gulf of Oman, lies between southeastern Iran and the Arabian Peninsula and opens into the Arabian Sea. The Persian Gulf is Iran's only means of access to the world's oceans and so has always been important economically and militarily.

CLIMATE

Iran's diverse geography contributes to a climate that is subject to extreme variation. For example, in the winter, most of the country experiences temperatures at or below freezing. In the summer, however, daytime temperatures can be as low as 35 degrees Fahrenheit in the mountains of the northwest but can run as high as 120 degrees Fahrenheit near the Persian Gulf coast and in the desert regions. Humidity also varies greatly: near 100 percent along the gulf coast but generally much lower in the interior. Rainfall totals vary widely from one region to another, ranging from less than two inches each year in the southeast to about eighty inches in the Caspian coastal plain in the north.

Tehran, located in northern Iran in the foothills of the Elburz Mountains, is subject to many of the extremes of the country's climate. Winters can be quite cold, averaging 36 degrees Fahrenheit in January, and snow can last until early March. On the other hand, the city is known for being hot and dry in the summer. However, only a short bus ride farther into the foothills of the Elburz Mountains, where a year-round cloud cover helps keep the summer temperatures lower than elsewhere in Iran, can bring relief from the summer's heat.

Tehran (pictured), situated between the Elburz Mountains and the Kavir Desert, is subject to many climatic extremes.

"THE GRANDEUR OF IRAN"

One of the classic descriptions of Iran's impressive landscape comes from Robert Byron's 1937 book *The Road to Oxiana.*

A burning dust-storm wafted us along the road to Khanikin. Through the murk loomed a line of hills. Christopher grasped my arm. "The ramparts of Iran!" he announced solemnly. A minute later we breasted a small incline and were on the flat again. This happened every five miles, till an oasis of sour green proclaimed the town and frontier. . . .

Then indeed the grandeur of Iran unfolded. Lit from behind by the fallen sun, and from in front by the rising moon, a vast panorama of rounded foothills rolled away from the Sassanian ruins, twinkling here and there with the amber lights of villages; till out of the far distance rose a mighty range of peaks, the real ramparts at last. Up and down we sped through the fresh tonic air, to the foot of the mountains; then up and up, to a pass between jagged pine-tufted pinnacles that mixed with the pattern of the stars.

The day's journey had a wild exhilaration. Up and down the mountains, over the endless flats, we bumped and swooped. The sun flayed us. Great spirals of dust, dancing like demons over the desert, stopped our dashing Chevrolet and choked us. Suddenly, from far across a valley, came the flash of a turquoise jar, bobbing along on a donkey. Its owner walked beside it, clad in a duller blue. And seeing the two lost in that gigantic stony waste, I understood why blue is the Persian colour, and why the Persian word for it means water as well.

In contrast to the extremes of winter and summer, the spring and fall are fairly mild in Iran. These two seasons tend to be short, however, according to the website operated by the Iranian embassy in Canada:

In Iran, the change from one season to the next is fairly abrupt. By 21 March, the beginning of the Iranian year (*Nowruz*), the fruit trees are in full bud and fresh green wheat covers the fields. Later, while the orchards are in bloom, wild flowers carpet the stony hills. Later, the summer heat burns and kills the flowers, and autumn is not marked by a display of bright colours and the soft haze of Indian summer; instead, there is a rapid transition from summer to winter.[5]

IRAN'S COMMUNITIES

Because of a more favorable climate, northern and western Iran are more densely populated than the arid eastern portion of the country. Four out of Iran's five largest cities—Tehran, Esfahan, Tabriz, and Shiraz—are located in the plateaus or the foothills of mountains. Only Mashhad, in the eastern highlands, is located outside the north and west mountain regions.

Iran's population has become steadily more settled and urbanized. For example, in 1966 there were an estimated 2 million nomads, but by the end of the twentieth century only about 240,000 people continued to live the nomadic lifestyle in the plains and the mountain pastures, migrating seasonally. And since the end of World War II, there has been a steady move from rural villages into cities, where 60 percent of Iran's population of roughly 66 million now lives. (Population estimates for Iran vary widely. Some authorities put the total population in 2001 as high as 73 million.)

No matter what type of community they live in, Iranians must deal with a land and climate that can often be harsh. Yet over the last several thousand years, the people of ancient Persia and modern Iran have proven themselves highly adaptable. It is this adaptability that has greatly enriched the heritage of the nation.

2

FROM PERSIA TO THE ISLAMIC REPUBLIC

The history of Iran—or Persia, as it was known until the 1930s—can be divided into two distinct time periods: pre-Islamic and Islamic. Iran's pre-Islamic period did much to define Iranian culture in later times. The strong and distinct Persian culture of the pre-Islamic period flourished for centuries and was never completely obscured by Islamic influence. Moreover, Persian culture has played an important role in shaping and defining Islam. Throughout history, the culture of Iran has been the product of the interplay between Persian and Islamic influences, and the spread and development of Islam in Iran has both complemented and conflicted with the nation's Persian heritage.

PRE-ISLAMIC DYNASTIES

For twelve centuries before the arrival of Islam in the seventh century A.D., Persia was ruled by four successive dynasties. These were the Achaemenian (559 to 330 B.C.), the Seleucid (312 to 190 B.C.), the Parthian (190 B.C. to A.D. 224), and the Sassanian (224 to 637). These four dynasties had common characteristics. According to Middle East expert Sandra Mackey, these characteristics were "the concepts of a powerful king ruling in the name of justice, the continuity of a distinct culture, and a sense of nationhood rooted more in cultural identity than in either government or territory."[6]

The four pre-Islamic dynasties were all Zoroastrian, the ancient Persian religion founded in the sixth century B.C. by the prophet Zoroaster. Zoroastrianism is monotheistic, meaning that it teaches that there is only one God, and emphasizes the responsibility of rulers to create a just and equitable society. These elements of Zoroastrianism are shared by Islam, the religion that came to Persia from Arabia in the seventh century.

THE ISLAMIC CONQUEST OF PERSIA

The Arab armies that began their conquest of the Persian Sassanian Empire in 636 were motivated by a desire to increase their own territory as well as to convert the Persians to their religion, Islam. Yazdegerd III, the last monarch of the Sassanian dynasty, escaped from the advancing Arab armies and tried to raise an army to fight the invaders. But in 642 the Sassanian army lost a decisive battle to the Arabs at Nahavand on the Iranian Plateau. How vigorously the Sassanians fought is open to question, since some writers at the time recorded that the Sassanian soldiers were so reluctant

A stone carving depicts monarchs of the Achaemenian dynasty, who ruled Persia from 559–330 B.C.

to fight that they had to be chained together. Indeed, as one historian points out, "the native populations had little to lose by cooperating with the conquering power. Moreover, the Muslims offered relative religious tolerance and fair treatment to populations that accepted Islamic rule without resistance."[7]

Zoroaster, pictured here, founded a monotheistic religion in Persia in the sixth century B.C.

THE LANGUAGE OF ISLAM

The impact of the Arab conquest during the seventh century is felt in Iran even today. In her book *Persian Mirrors*, American writer Elaine Sciolino describes the difficulty Iranians have had with the fact that Arabic, rather than Persian, is the language of their nation's predominant religion.

It sometimes seemed difficult for the Islamic Republic to reconcile itself to the fact that the language of Islam is not Persian, but Arabic. I was amused by a speech that Ayatollah Khamenei gave one day to an international conference on the Persian language. He noted that Islam was introduced to Iran in Arabic, but added that it was "promoted" through Persian. Arabic is a particularly difficult language to learn, and many students resent the fact that they have to study it at all. (Seven years of Arabic are required of all Iranian students.) The vast majority never master the language and thus have no idea what the clerics are saying when they recite the Koran [the holy book of Islam] from pulpits or television screens.

Despite the cooperation they received from the people, the Arabs set about obliterating the Persian culture. The Arabs replaced the Sassanian language, known as Pahlavi, with Arabic. They also demolished Sassanian buildings and even entire cities. The conquerors took works of art made of silver and gold and melted them down to make coins.

Despite the destruction, Persian culture survived. According to Mackey, "When Iran fell to the Arabs in the seventh century, Persian culture stayed intact to fertilize Islam and define it for Iran."[8] The Persians made significant contributions to all branches of Islamic life and letters and helped define Islam for the rest of the world. Mackey writes,

Tolerant of diversity, quick to absorb from others that which was of value, the Iranians undertook the Persian conquest of Islam. With Iranian intellectuals as the conduit, the Islamic Empire drew together the learning of Greece and India as well as the areas in between. From 813 to 833, the Persians within the House of Wisdom [a translation center and library] established by the Caliph Mamun translated Aristotle, Plato, Euclid, Ptolemy,

Archimedes, and Hippocrates into Arabic and added to them the scientific works of Persia and India. While Europe remained mired in the Dark Ages, emissaries from Islam's caliph went out over the [Islamic] empire in search of literature, philosophy, theology, and science to be translated into Arabic under formal Arabic grammar largely devised by an Iranian scholar named Sibveyh.[9]

As was their practice elsewhere, the Arab conquerors spread their religion throughout Persia and replaced the Persians' ancient religion of Zoroastrianism with Islam. But even in the religious sphere, Persian culture did not yield altogether. For example, archaeologists have pointed out that builders of mosques adopted some of the architecture of Zoroastrian temples.

For their part, although becoming Muslims required the Persians to adapt to Arab cultural traditions, that adaptation was not necessarily difficult. Even though most of the native population did not convert to Islam until the ninth century, according to Mackey,

This religious conversion came easily to the Iranians in part because Islam carried within it elements of their

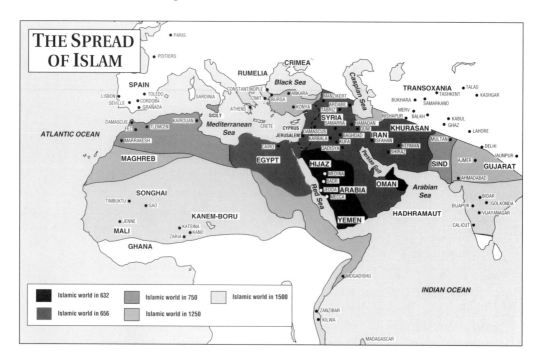

THE SPREAD OF ISLAM

Islamic world in 632
Islamic world in 656
Islamic world in 750
Islamic world in 1250
Islamic world in 1500

own pre-Islamic beliefs: monotheism; the fear of evil; the existence of angels; and the acceptance of Judgment Day. . . . Finally there was Islam's promise of justice, the well-spring of authority in Persia since the reign of Cyrus. Thus through the Iranians' gradual transition from Zoroastrianism to Islam much of the essence and religious character of Iranian identity remained intact. Religion stayed central to existence; Allah replaced Ahura Mazda; Muhammad substituted for Zoroaster as the spiritual force sent into a world full of evil and injustice to lead the cosmic battle for goodness and compassion.[10]

THE SAFAVID DYNASTY

The relative ease with which the nation converted to Islam did not, however, make Persia immune to conflict. From the eleventh through the fifteenth centuries, Islamic Persia faced another series of invasions. It was overrun first by the Seljuq Turks, a nomadic tribe originally from the plains of Central Asia, and then by the Mongols and Timurids from the East. During this time, Persia suffered from numerous rebellions and civil wars as well. These centuries of upheaval were followed by the rise of the Safavid dynasty, the first native Iranian dynasty to come to power in a thousand years. The dynasty began in 1501 when the Safavids, under the leadership of Esmail I, seized power in Tabriz and made it their capital. Esmail then declared himself shah, or king, of Persia.

The Safavids' rise to power had far-reaching effects on the Persians' religion. The Safavids were followers of Shia Islam, the minority branch of the religion. Although Persia had been predominantly Muslim for several centuries, it was not until the sixteenth century that Shia Islam officially became the state religion under Shah Esmail I. The Safavids then began to convert the largely Sunni majority in Iran to the Shia sect. This move would have long-term consequences. According to Mackey, "In declaring Shiism the state religion, the Safavid dynasty began the process by which Iran would be defined by Shia theology as well as Persian culture."[11]

The two centuries of Safavid rule in Persia were characterized by intermittent warfare with neighboring countries. The dynasty came to an end in 1722 when a Sunni Muslim

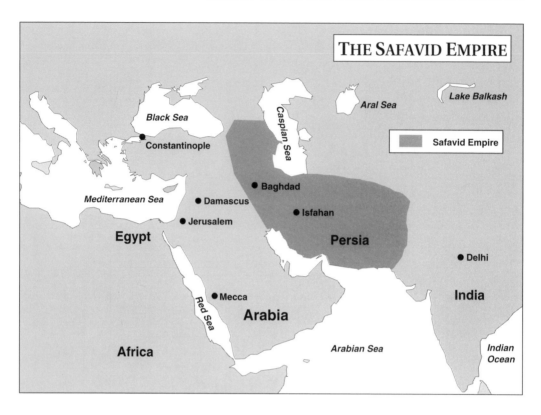

THE SAFAVID EMPIRE

army from Afghanistan invaded Persia and executed the last Safavid shah. For the remainder of the eighteenth century, Persia was plunged into a state of general disorder and anarchy. In the absence of any strong central authority, tribal groups that had until then been on the periphery of society came to dominate. First, a group called the Zands took control of much of Iran, ruling from 1750 to 1794, but they were challenged and eventually defeated by a Turkish-speaking tribe known as the Qajars. The Qajar leader Agha Muhammad declared himself master of the country, reestablishing the monarchy in the process.

THE QAJAR DYNASTY AND THE CONSTITUTIONAL REVOLUTION

Agha Muhammad Shah proved to be a cruel and capricious ruler, and he was assassinated by his own servants after ruling for only a year. Agha Muhammad's successor was his nephew, Fath Ali, who wanted to make a complete break from his family's tribal past and reinstituted the Persian monarchy in all its splendor. Fath Ali Shah, who ruled from 1797 to 1834, reestablished the partnership between the monarchy and the Shia hierarchy. This meant that the Muslim clergy had authority over religious law and the collection of religious taxes, and even had small private armies to help enforce their religious judgments. For his part, the shah's cooperation with the clergy gave him legitimacy as the divinely appointed ruler of Persia.

The reestablishment of the monarchy did not guarantee Persian autonomy, however. During the nineteenth century, two great world powers, Britain and Russia, began to dominate Persia's trade, interfere with its internal affairs, and vie for control of the country. Nasir ad-Din, the Qajar shah from 1848 to 1896, asked Britain for protection against Russian incursions into northern Persia; in return, Britain asked the shah for trade concessions. For example, in 1890 the shah granted the British Imperial Tobacco Company the exclusive right to buy the entire tobacco crop of Persia. This decision meant that many thousands of tobacco growers and merchants no longer had control over the price of their products, and this led to a popular revolt, forcing the shah to revoke the concession.

The revolt over the tobacco concession would not be the last time that public discontent would lead to demands for change in Persia. Less than two decades later, a combination of royal and bureaucratic corruption, oppression of the rural population, and concern over foreign influence led the people of Persia to demand that some restrictions be placed on the power of the shah. The shah's failure to respond to these growing protests and demands for reform in turn led to the Constitutional Revolution of 1906. In October of that year, an elected assembly drew up a constitution that limited royal power and set up a legislative assembly called the Majlis.

Instituting these reforms failed to bring stability to Iran. Shah Muzaffar ad-Din died five days after the constitution took effect; two years later, Muzaffar's successor, Shah Muhammad Ali, attempted to regain absolute control of the country. He disbanded the Majlis and arrested many of its members. Despite these moves, the shah was deposed by constitutional forces and forced into exile in Russia. His young son Ahmad then became shah under the guidance of a regent.

Shah Ahmad was the last shah of the Qajar dynasty. Ahmad was overthrown by Reza Khan, who changed the country's name to Iran.

The new constitution also did not put an end to foreign interference in Persia. In 1907, Britain and Russia divided Persia into spheres of economic and political influence, with the Russians controlling the northern part of the country and the British controlling the south and east. During World War I (1914–1918), Persia was occupied by Russian and British troops. Russian influence greatly diminished in 1917, however, when Russia became embroiled in its own revolution. But British influence in the country's affairs continued for several decades.

For a time, Britain's control of Iran was extensive. Shah Ahmad had little real power, and in 1919 the Anglo-Persian Treaty established Persia as a British protectorate. The British military continued its occupation of the country after World War I and controlled the Persian oil industry. However, British control was interrupted by a coup d'état in 1921 led by a little-known Persian colonel named Reza Khan.

THE PAHLAVI ERA

Reza Khan quickly established control over Persia. In 1923 he became prime minister; then in late 1925 the Majlis designated him shah, establishing a new dynasty. He chose the name Reza Shah Pahlavi. In 1935, Reza Shah changed the country's name from Persia to Iran. The name *Iran* means "land of the Aryans" and was meant to evoke the time when an Indo-European tribe known as the Aryans began migrating to the area around the Iranian Plateau in about 1000 B.C. The nation's new name reflected Reza Shah's interest in the pre-Islamic era and the country's ancient religion of Zoroastrianism. According to historian Sandra Mackey,

Reza Shah decided to bypass Islam by connecting the notion of modern Iran to a glorified image of ancient Persia. To this end, he summoned the impotent nation once more to the great days of Iranian history. . . . In his resurrection of pre-Islamic Iran, Reza Shah fertilized the deeply planted idea that the Arabs humiliated Iran in the seventh century and plowed up images of ignorant camel herders compelling the highly civilized Iranians to accept a new religion. He fed it all with a systematic resuscitation of Zoroastrian symbols, congenial to the spirit of denying the relevance of Islam.[12]

The name that Reza Shah adopted for himself was similarly meant to evoke the country's pre-Islamic past, since Pahlavi was the language spoken by the Sassanians. In addition, Reza Shah revived the Sassanian title *shahanshah*, or king of kings, for himself.

Reza Shah, pictured here, strove to modernize and Westernize Iran during his fifteen-year rule.

Though the shah wanted to evoke the glories of ancient Persia, he also wanted to bring Iran into the modern age. He felt that the best way to do this was by imitating the West and minimizing Islamic influence. He replaced the country's Muslim laws with a civil system and suppressed Muslim celebrations and holidays. According to author Robin Wright,

During his fifteen-year rule, Reza Shah was particularly contemptuous of religion: Islamic judges, taxes and laws were secularized, their replacements based on European models. Traditional parts of old Tehran were plowed to make way for paved boulevards and modern buildings. Islamic schools, the primary source of education in many corners of the country, were put under a

A REMINDER OF PAHLAVI REPRESSION

The last shah of Iran, Muhammad Reza Shah Pahlavi, had many grand palaces built for himself and his family at a time when many of his people lived in poverty. After the revolution, some of these empty palaces were simply abandoned, while others were turned into museums to showcase the excesses of the Pahlavis. A Canadian author named Alison Wearing and her companion broke into one of the shah's palaces, abandoned since the revolution, during a trip they made to Iran in the mid-1990s. In her book *Honeymoon in Purdah*, Wearing describes the repression and injustices perpetrated by the shah during his reign that came to an end with the Islamic Revolution.

It has been almost twenty years since the Shah was here. Almost twenty years since he was driven from his country in disgrace; since the streets filled with demonstrators demanding an end to the injustices in their country: the concentration of wealth in the hands of so few, foreign domination of oil resources, military spending that amounted to a quarter of the national budget, censorship and the rule of fear by the Shah's security service, persecution of religious and political figures, saturation of the country in American values.

It has been almost twenty years since the Shah answered peaceful demonstrations by ordering his security forces to fire on the protestors, killing dozens; since the demonstrations grew into riots, and the Shah answered by ordering his troops to fire into the crowds, killing hundreds; since a political exile by the name of Khomeini encouraged the demonstrators not to give up their fight against injustice, and the Shah answered by ordering his security forces to fire into the throngs that had gathered on the day of communal prayer, killing thousands.

We walk from room to room in silence.

Echoes of laughter—the quaint titter of the wealthy—bleed from the ceilings. It is the sort of laughter fuelled not by happiness, but by pride; the pride that comes with being king, shahanshah, king of kings. The pride that allows a man to rob his own people. And not think himself a criminal.

government ministry and their curricula secularized and standardized, often on European models.[13]

The shah even prohibited women from wearing traditional Islamic clothing, but this decision met considerable resistance. For example, although soldiers forcibly removed veils from women who wore them in public, many persisted in doing so. One man recalls, "My mother refused to take off her chador [traditional Muslim head covering]. . . . When she and her sister wanted to go to the baths, because there was none at home, they had friends in the street signal them when there were no police. Then they ran swiftly to the bathhouse so they wouldn't be caught with their chadors. My mother was very staunch."[14]

Reza Shah's attempts at modernization and Westernization were carried further by his son and successor, Muhammad Reza Shah Pahlavi. During the 1950s and 1960s, illiteracy was reduced, health services were improved, mass industrialization was begun, and women were given the right to vote. Western influence in Iran was evident in dress, music, films, and television programs.

AYATOLLAH RUHOLLAH KHOMEINI

The rapid changes instituted by Muhammad Reza Shah led to internal conflicts. During the 1960s and 1970s, many people felt that the influence of the West—particularly the United States—was a threat to their country's Islamic and Iranian

A national hero in Iran, Ruhollah Khomeini (center) publicly opposed Iran's shah for his close ties to the United States. Khomeini was exiled by the shah in 1965.

cultural values and identity. One leading critic of the shah was an ayatollah (a Shiite scholar) named Ruhollah Khomeini, who publicly accused the shah of corruption, violations of the constitution, election rigging, and attempting to destroy Islam. Khomeini became a national hero when his outspoken opposition led the shah to order his arrest in June 1963. Eventually, the shah exiled Khomeini, who went to live in Turkey, then in Iraq, and finally in France.

Nothing the shah tried silenced Khomeini. From outside the country, Khomeini maintained contact with his former students in Iran and became accepted as a leader by other groups who opposed the shah. Khomeini wanted to do more than remove Muhammad Reza Shah Pahlavi from office, however; he also had a plan for an Islamic government, one led by clerics, in Iran.

The shah had other opponents who, for their own reasons, backed Khomeini. Middle-class bureaucrats, teachers, lawyers, and doctors, many of them secularists (those who preferred that religion have little to do with government), wanted Iran to be a true democracy. And, like many who followed Khomeini, these secular opponents resented the shah's close ties to the United States.

The shah responded by having his opponents arrested, tortured, exiled, and even executed. He had created SAVAK, an intelligence and security agency, in 1957, and in the 1970s SAVAK increasingly carried out brutal repression on those opposed to the shah. Yet even as political repression in Iran grew more severe, opposition to the shah's regime solidified.

THE ISLAMIC REVOLUTION

The shah responded to his opponents with increasing force, but his hold on power grew more tenuous. After a year of demonstrations that turned into riots in which many people were killed, the shah finally boarded a plane and fled Iran on January 16, 1979. Two weeks later, the Ayatollah Khomeini returned from his fourteen-year exile and took control of the country. That April, Iranians voted in favor of a constitution establishing an Islamic republic, and they chose Khomeini as their *faqih*, or supreme leader. The official name of the country became the Islamic Republic of Iran.

A new constitution was ratified in the autumn of 1979. Author Robin Wright explains how the constitution helped es-

Khomeini supporters gather in Tehran in celebration of the Islamic Revolution.

tablish Iran as a thoroughly Islamic state by reshaping the government's structure: "The most important change was at the top. The presidency was weakened to titular status—to avoid a strong head of government creating a new dynasty, as had happened with the first Pahlavi king. Real leadership was instead invested in a Supreme Leader."[15] To help safeguard and implement the changes brought by the revolution, Khomeini abolished SAVAK and established a new security force known as the Revolutionary Guards.

After the revolution, Iran returned to a more conservative and traditional Islamic way of life. Western influences that had been encouraged by the two Pahlavi shahs were eradicated. Robin Wright explains some of these changes:

> Cultural outlets were forcibly closed. University life was suspended while curriculum was reviewed. Bars and nightclubs had their liquor stocks destroyed before being boarded up. Religious vigilantes monitored morality in each neighborhood. Streets were often empty at night, because pedestrians and drivers wanted to avoid searches at impromptu checkpoints set up by the new Revolutionary Guards.

> Even fashion changed. Women were forced behind chadors and *hejab*, the generic term for a variety of body covers. Many simply retreated to their homes. To show loyalty, men grew beards or a permanent three-day stubble. Ties, the epitome of Western style, became taboo.[16]

Islamic women cloaked in chadors. The law in Iran requires women to be covered from head to toe while in public.

THE BASIJ OF THE IRAN-IRAQ WAR

In September 1980, Iraq invaded Iran's oil-rich western province of Khuzestan and sparked the Iran-Iraq War, which was to last eight years. The long, bloody war cost the lives of 500,000 individuals on each side and left about 5 million Iranians without homes or jobs. The war also saw the creation of the military force known as the Basij in Iran. Christiane Bird describes the Basij in her book, *Neither East nor West.*

To the West, the most astonishing aspect of the Iran-Iraq War was the Iranians' willingness to martyr themselves. Iraq was much better equipped militarily, with a well-disciplined army and sophisticated weapons, but Iran had tens of thousands of believers ready to die in battle against the blasphemous Arab infidels. In addition to the regular Iranian army and the Revolutionary Guards, there was also the Basij, composed mostly of teenage volunteers who enrolled through more than 9,000 mosques across the country, often for short periods such as summer vacations. Recognizable by their red or yellow headbands declaring the greatness of Khomeini or Allah, the Basij-is came primarily from a working-class or peasant background; the name of their organization, Basij-e Mustazafin, means "Mobilization of the Deprived." In the early years of the war, the Basij-is became famous for running ahead of the Revolutionary Guards to detonate land mines. Their elders often tried to stop them, but the boys believed that their deaths guaranteed them a place in paradise, and some died wearing a plastic key around their necks—the key to heaven. Later, that kind of extreme fervor died down, but the Iranian armed forces were still able to rely largely on volunteer recruits until the final year of the war.

ISOLATION AND WAR

Khomeini's wish that Western influences in general and American influence in particular be minimized was soon translated into reality. On November 4, 1979, four hundred Revolutionary Guards and Iranian students stormed and seized the U.S. embassy in Tehran, taking sixty-six American diplomats hostage. The protesters demanded that the deposed shah, who had been granted entry into the United States the previous month for medical treatment, be extradited to Iran and that Iranian assets that were frozen in U.S. banks be unfrozen immediately. What started as a student demonstration was quickly seized upon by Ayatollah Khomeini as an opportunity to diminish the U.S. interference in Iranian political affairs; the embassy takeover had official sanction after a couple of days. The already strained ties between Iran and the United States were broken altogether during the hostage crisis, which lasted more than a year. Mutual hostility and mistrust would characterize relations between the two nations for decades to come.

Even while the hostage crisis was still under way, a far more destructive crisis was brewing. Seeing an opportunity in Iran's internal turmoil, the leader of neighboring Iraq, Saddam Hussein, launched an invasion of the oil-rich provinces in western Iran in 1980. Hussein harbored more than a desire for Iran's oil. He also hoped to keep the Islamic Revolution from spreading to Iraq. Western countries and the former Soviet Union sided with Iraq during the war that followed because the Islamic Revolution and the U.S. hostage crisis had left many nations mistrustful of Iran.

An Iranian soldier keeps watch at his post during the Iran-Iraq War.

A Martyr's Funeral

The tulip is not only the national flower of Iran but also the symbol of martyrdom. Iran is proud of its martyrs, especially those who died fighting in the bloody and protracted war with Iraq. At the Martyr's Museum in Tehran, display cases are lined up in rows. Each display case is dedicated to one or two martyrs and contains torn or bloodied clothing, other personal effects, and a red plastic tulip. In her book *The Last Great Revolution*, Robin Wright describes a funeral procession that took place in Iran during the early 1980s. The deceased was a soldier who had been killed in the war and elevated to the status of martyr.

> I still remember the first funeral cortege I saw en route to the graveyard named after the prophet Mohammad's daughter. It was led by a green hatchback. Two men sitting in the open rear were running a large tape recorder from which a man's chanting of Koranic verses was amplified on two loudspeakers strapped to the car roof. On the hood, a garland of flowers surrounded a picture of the deceased soldier. A beige ambulance carrying the body was next. Its back doors were open and young men, probably family members and fellow soldiers, were crowded on both sides of the body. Buses packed with relatives and friends followed. One was plastered with a large banner reading, "Congratulations on your martyrdom."

The Iran-Iraq War quickly turned into a stalemate, but an extremely bloody one. Fierce land battles as well as air and missile attacks on each other's cities and oil installations left hundreds of thousands of Iranians and Iraqis dead and many more disabled and homeless. The war also caused enormous damage to the infrastructure of both nations. Eventually, after eight years of fighting, the two nations agreed to a negotiated cease-fire in 1988 and a return to their prewar borders, with neither side achieving a clear victory.

Iran After Khomeini

The Ayatollah Khomeini died in 1989, not long after the Iran-Iraq War ended. In his place, conservative cleric Ayatollah Ali Khamenei was selected as the new supreme leader, and Hashemi Rafsanjani became president. Some of

President Muhammad Khatami addresses the people of Iran.

the more restrictive regulations imposed in the early days of the Islamic Republic began to be eased. In 1997 this trend continued as reformist Muhammad Khatami was elected president, and when he was reelected in 2001. Although he is the son of a renowned cleric and himself a *hojjat-ol-eslam* ("proof of Islam," a rank below that of ayatollah) and a *seyyed* (a descendant of Muhammad), Khatami found that many of his reforms were blocked by Supreme Leader Ayatollah Khamenei and the Council of Guardians.

Since the revolution, there have been periods in which religion-based restrictions on civil liberties were strictly enforced and other times when enforcement has been relaxed. But at all times, Islam has played a huge role in every aspect of life in Iran—as it has since the seventh century.

RELIGION IN IRAN

Iran is an Islamic republic, which means that there is little separation between politics, business, and religion. From the highest levels of government to the daily lives of individuals, all aspects of life are tied together by Shia Islam. The supreme political leader must also be a Muslim cleric, and even though Iran has an elected president and legislative assembly, the Council of Guardians, which is composed mostly of religious scholars, can and often does overrule the actions of officials in the other branches of government. Regardless of their personal beliefs, all Iranians are expected to live in a way that does not violate the government's interpretation of Islam.

When the Islamic Republic of Iran was established in 1979, many devout Muslims thought that a new era had begun and that their nation would be blessed by God. But instead of peace and prosperity, they experienced continued turmoil, internal dissension, and conflict with Western nations, the Soviet Union, and even their Muslim neighbors. Their unmet expectations and the tactics the government has used to respond to the problems have had wide-ranging effects on the role of Islam in the lives of the Iranian people.

ISLAM IN IRAN

Islam, which has been the dominant religion in Iran for over thirteen hundred years, began in Arabia, across the Persian Gulf to the southwest of Iran, in the early seventh century. In the city of Mecca, a merchant named Muhammad began receiving what he said were revelations from God. The revelations called on Muhammad to tell the Arab peoples to stop worshiping the many gods of their tribal religion and submit completely to the will of one God, the same God worshiped by Jews and Christians. At first, only Muhammad's family and

Muhammad, the founder of Islam, leads his followers into battle. The new community of Muslims saw Muhammad not only as a prophet but also as their political and military leader.

friends believed that the revelations were truly from God, but within a few years, thousands of people had joined him. The revelations encouraged Muhammad and his new followers to create a just society and to oppose any nation that did not accept the revelations Muhammad had received.

The revelations were eventually written down and compiled into the sacred book of Islam, the Qur'an. Muslims rely on the Qur'an for guidance, but it is not regarded as a complete answer book. Muslims also look to Muhammad's customary behavior, known as the sunna of the Prophet, for more detailed instructions. From the Qur'an and the sunna came five essential practices, known as the Five Pillars of Islam. They are the profession of faith, in which Muslims acknowledge that there is only one God and that Muhammad is his prophet; praying five times daily in a prescribed manner; paying an annual tax for the benefit of the poor; fasting from dawn to dusk during the Islamic month of Ramadan; and if circumstances permit, making a pilgrimage to Mecca during the month of Dhu 'l-Hijja once during a Muslim's lifetime.

SHIA ISLAM

Though all Muslims agree on the Five Pillars, there is a split within Islam dating almost to the time of Muhammad that has profound implications for Iranians. Muhammad died in 632 without leaving specific instructions for who his successor, or caliph, should be. Some thought that the caliph should be chosen from among Muhammad's close companions on the basis of maturity, wisdom, and devotion to Islam. Others believed that Muhammad had chosen his closest male relative, his cousin and son-in-law Ali ibn Abi Talib, as his successor. Ali was passed over the first three times a caliph was chosen but was selected to be the fourth caliph in 656.

However, not everyone recognized Ali's right to be caliph even then. A bitter struggle ensued, ending in Ali's death by assassination in 661. The majority of Muslims followed the victor in the conflict, Muawiyah, who became the fifth

Practicing one of the Five Pillars of Islam, Muslim men face toward Mecca in prayer.

caliph. Nevertheless, a significant minority insisted that Ali had been the legitimate successor to Muhammad and that only Ali's descendants could become leaders in the future. This minority became known as the Shia (party) of Ali.

The dispute between the Sunni (the Muslim majority) and Shia was not only over who would lead the Muslim community but what that leadership entailed. The Sunni believed that the caliph assumed Muhammad's political but not religious role. That is, the Sunni caliphs headed the Muslim state, but religious matters were left to the scholars, those who had studied the Qur'an and sunna extensively and had demonstrated an understanding of the principles of Islam. The Shii, on the other hand, believed that their leaders, known as imams, were spiritual as well as political guides, that even though they were not prophets as Muhammad had been, they were divinely inspired and authoritative interpreters of the Qur'an.

The majority of Iranians (about 89 percent) are Shia Muslims, and virtually all belong to the *Ithna Ashari* or Twelver sect. The name comes from their belief that there were twelve legitimate imams following Muhammad's death. The twelfth imam, Muhammad al-Muntazar, was still a child when he disappeared in 874 and became known as the Hidden Imam. Twelver Shiites await the return of the Hidden Imam as the Mahdi, or "rightly guided one," who they say will usher in a worldwide reign of justice and peace.

Traditionally, the Shia thought that the only proper leader of an Islamic government would be the Hidden Imam himself. But Khomeini taught that it was possible for someone other than the Hidden Imam to assume the reigns of government, and he became the first individual to do so. Many Iranians believe that in some way Khomeini was in fact the Hidden Imam, and after his return to Iran he became known as Imam Khomeini, giving him a religious and political importance in the Shia world unprecedented in modern times. Khomeini's life and ideas have continued to influence the religious life of the country since his death in 1989. Pictures of him are everywhere in Iran, from billboards to murals on the walls of buildings to portraits in homes and offices. His books are still widely read, and politicians and religious leaders often justify their policies by saying that they are attempting to carry forward Khomeini's legacy.

THE STUDY OF ISLAM

In the Islamic Republic, many young Iranian men aspire to become ayatollahs, experts in Islamic law. In her book *Black on Black*, author Ana Briongos explains that the experience of these theology students varies greatly from one man to the next.

The study of Islam can last a lifetime. Some students stay for six years, others for twelve, twenty, even thirty. The many subjects they study include Arabic, grammar, logic, rhetoric, literature, Islamic philosophy, law and jurisprudence. There is no predetermined syllabus, nor are there any exams. Each student needs a different amount of time to become an expert in the interpretation of holy books, and together the teacher and student work out how long it will take. As the years go by, the student has opportunities to see whether or not he is capable of holding his own in a high-level theological discussion, conducted in the esoteric language he has been struggling to learn, not just with his master and guide, but also with other eminent theologians. It will be obvious to him when he has gone as far as he can. If he comes up against a barrier his intellect will never penetrate, however many years he spends trying, it's time to quit. For the duration of his studies, the student lives at the expense of the theologian, who gives him shelter, food and even sometimes a small allowance. With time, he will become a mullah, and if he is a brilliant student, an *ayatollah*. The young men who choose to go to *madrasés* [Islamic schools] know that they are choosing a life of austerity, without material rewards, although they do acquire great prestige. In the last hundred years, all the great theologians have studied at Ghom, or at the other great center of Shi'ite learning, Najaf in Iraq, where Ali, the son-in-law of the Prophet, is buried. It was here in Ghom that Khomeini dispensed his teachings before he was expelled from the country by the Shah, and it was here that he came to live when he returned to Iran.

THE ROLE OF ISLAM IN PUBLIC AND PRIVATE LIFE

For many Muslims in Iran, life is lived in expectation of an afterlife, and every act can be classified according to its value for getting one into heaven. According to religion scholar Moojan Momen,

Iranian men brandish photos of Islamic leaders, including the late Ayatollah Khomeini.

Life for the devout Shi'i is perceived very much as having an account with God. This account is credited and debited during one's life. At death, for those with a sufficiently large positive balance in their account there is heaven; for those with a large negative balance there is hell; and for those in between there is the in-between world of *barzakh* (purgatory) where they are punished for their sins sufficiently to make them eventually worthy of heaven.[17]

Among Muslims, there are five classes of behavior: obligatory, desirable, neutral, undesirable, and forbidden. One earns credit by doing what is obligatory or desirable and refraining from what is undesirable or forbidden. One can also earn credit by performing acts of charity, known as *thawab*, which vary in their value depending on the nature of the act. One is debited by failing to do what is obligatory and by doing what is forbidden (*haram*). Doing what is neutral or undesirable or refraining from what is neutral or desirable produces no change in the account.

Most people require guidance in understanding this complex system of debits and credits, and this instruction usually comes from the local mullah, the scholar who runs the mosque and officiates at the daily and Friday prayers and other observances. The mullah is seen as more than a source of information, however: He is also regarded as a link to God. According to Momen,

> Whereas in Sunni Islam there is a direct relationship between the believer and God as revealed in the religion of Islam, in Shi'i Islam there is something of a triangular relationship. While for some things, such as the daily obligatory prayers, the individual is in direct relationship to God, in other matters he looks (usually through

THE EDUCATION OF THE MULLAHS

Iran and Islam are often portrayed by Westerners as rigid and unyielding. Some observers are surprised to learn that one of the key skills taught to Shii clerics is debate. Elaine Sciolino explains this concept in her book *Persian Mirrors*.

> Contrary to the perception outside Iran that religious truth is monolithic and that dissent is not tolerated, one of the defining traits of Shiism is its emphasis on argument. Clerics are encouraged and expected to challenge interpretations of the Koran, even those of the most learned ayatollahs, in the hope that new and better interpretations may emerge. It is a concept little grasped in the West, but it is critical to understanding Iran's current reformers and their leader President Khatami, who is the son of one of the most revered—and liberal-minded—of the ayatollahs in pre-revolutionary Iran.

the mediation of the local mullah) to the *marja' at-taqlid* [source of imitation] who is regarded as being in a more direct relationship with God.[18]

In Shia Islam, each person should be under the direction of a *mujtahid*, a scholar deemed competent to guide the faithful in all matters of religious law and practice. Submitting to the direction of the *mujtahid* is known as *taqlid*, or imitation. Some Shii scholars believe that without *taqlid*, religious observances are invalid, even if they are otherwise done correctly.

Much of the practice of Islam is performed in public. For example, the profession of faith by which one becomes a Muslim must be said before two witnesses, and the daily prayers should be said in the presence of others whenever possible. According to Momen,

> The result of this concentration on the externals of the religion is that in tight-knit social groups such as the Bazaar [the people who run the central market areas of Iranian cities], one's piety and religious merit are judged by others not on the basis of one's beliefs (which are indeed seldom discussed) but on the basis of being observed to be performing the required rituals.[19]

THE PRACTICE OF ISLAM

One of the primary rhythms of life in Iran is the five-times-daily Islamic prayer, the *salat*. All over Iran, the call to prayer (*adhan*) goes out from the minarets of mosques through loudspeakers at sunset, late evening, morning, noon, and midafternoon.

Before prayer, Muslims must be ritually clean. All mosques have fountains or other facilities where worshipers can wash before prayer, performing what is known as the minor ablution. Some types of impurity require a more extensive cleansing, however. According to religion scholars Sachiko Murata and William Chittick,

> There are two main categories of impurity, and two basic kinds of ablution to remove impurity. The major ablution (*ghusl*) is required after sexual intercourse or emission of semen, menstruation, childbirth, and touching a human corpse. A person in need of a major

A muslim cleric raises his hands in prayer.

ablution cannot perform the ritual prayer and should not enter a mosque or touch the Koran [another spelling of Qur'an]. In order to perform the *salat*, one has to be free from minor impurity as well. This kind of impurity occurs if one sleeps, goes to the toilet, breaks wind, and in certain other ways as well. It is removed by a minor ablution (*wudu*).

The major ablution involves washing the whole body from head to toe, making sure that every part of it gets wet. The minor ablution involves rinsing or wiping the following with water, in this order: the hands, the mouth, the nose, the right and left forearms, the face, the head, the ears, and the right and left feet.[20]

The required prayers take only a few minutes to perform. The prayers include recitations of the profession of faith, the Fatihah (the seven-verse-long first chapter of the Qur'an), other verses from the Qur'an, and blessings for Muhammad and the Muslim community, all performed along with a prescribed set of postures and hand gestures. They are followed by formal greetings for one's fellow worshipers. The form and content of the daily prayers originated with Muhammad. According to Murata and Chittick,

> Although the Koran repeatedly commands Muslims to perform the *salat*, it says little about what the *salat* actually involves. How to perform the *salat* was taught by the Prophet, and thus Muslims today, wherever they live, pray in essentially the same way that Muhammad prayed and taught them to pray.[21]

FRIDAY PRAYERS

While visiting Iran in 1998, American Christiane Bird attended Friday prayers with her Iranian friend Lona at the University of Tehran. Bird describes the experience in her book *Neither East nor West*. The prayers were held outdoors, and men and women sat in separate groups. Bird writes that at the sound of the words "There is no God but Allah and Muhammad is His Prophet,"

> the women all stood and pulled their *chadors* down farther over their faces, until they resembled a field full of mummies. Lona and I were the only women in sight wearing *manteaus* and *rusaris*, not *chadors*, and I was the only woman not beginning to pray. *Allahu akbar, Allahu akbar*—God is great, God is great. The women cupped their hands to their ears, symbolic of hearing the message of God, and then stood with their heads bowed and their hands by their sides, silently reciting verses from the Qor'an. Next, all bent forward from the waist, in a long bow with their hands on their knees, then stood again, and knelt with their foreheads to their prayer stones on the ground. "Glory to God, glory to God," a low rumble rose up from the men's side, washing over the hundreds of motionless, whispering black and white turtle backs at my feet; men are supposed to say their prayers out loud, whereas women must whisper. I caught my breath at the moment's power—and beauty. *Islam* means "submission," as in submission to God, and for the first time I caught a glimmering of what that meant. All these thousands of worshippers, united by their belief in a higher good.

*A muslim man
performs his ablutions
outside of a mosque.*

Muslims in Iran are required to attend the Friday noon prayer, which includes a sermon by the leader of each mosque, and so it is the most important prayer time of the week. This is true for all branches of Islam, but it is especially so in Iran because the nation is an Islamic republic. In fact, even prior to the Islamic Revolution, the Friday sermons in Iran often had great political as well as religious significance.

THE ISLAMIC REPUBLIC AND RELIGIOUS DIVERSITY

Many Iranians are deeply religious—their faith is the center of their lives. However, not all these people are Shia Muslims. Members of a variety of other religions live in the country as well, including Christians (about 300,000), Jews (about 50,000), and Zoroastrians (about 32,000). These religious groups are officially recognized in the Iranian constitution, and seats in parliament are set aside for members of these faiths.

In addition to Christians, Jews, and Zoroastrians, there are more than 300,000 adherents of the Baha'i Faith in Iran. The Baha'i Faith began in Iran, but because it teaches that a new

Muslims at the Friday noon prayer, the most important prayer time of the week.

revelation from God should take the place of Islam it is the one religion that is legally restricted in the country. The movement that became the Baha'i Faith began in 1844 when a young merchant named Sayyed Ali Muhammad Shirazi adopted the title of the Bab (gate) and began to teach that the era of Islam was at an end. The Bab sent out disciples to many cities in Iran and surrounding countries to proclaim his message, and within two years he had several thousand followers, known as Babis, including some Muslim scholars. The Bab and his followers soon experienced several years of persecution by the Persian government, including the execution of the Bab himself in 1850. A group of Babis plotted to avenge his death in 1852, but their plan was discovered, leading to a new round of persecutions and the deaths of most of the leaders of the Babi movement.

One leader of the Babis who was not killed, however, was Mirza Husayn Ali Nuri. While in prison, he had a vision in which he was told that he was to be the next prophet, carrying on the revelation begun by the Bab. After he was released from prison, he spent several years in exile, and in 1863 he announced that he was the prophet the Bab had predicted would come. He adopted the name Baha'ullah (the Glory of God). The religion he founded is known today as the Baha'i Faith. It teaches the unity of all humankind and advocates for peace and justice.

Although the Baha'i Faith forbids revolutionary activity, like the Babis in the nineteenth century, the Baha'is today are subject to persecution. Since 1983, the Baha'i Faith has been officially banned in the Islamic Republic, and Baha'is are under intense legal and economic pressure. Their marriages and divorces are not legally recognized, and they are

A Zoroastrian woman presents an offering. Although predominantly Muslim, Iran is home to people of a number of faiths.

THE RIGHT PATH

Abdul Karim Soroush is Iran's best-known philosopher and an outspoken advocate for reform in Iran. His views are often controversial, and include the beliefs that there is no one correct way to interpret religion and that Islam can be compatible with both democracy and modernity. In 1998, author Robin Wright interviewed Soroush after he had returned to Iran from two years in exile. In her book *The Last Great Revolution*, Wright recorded Soroush's views about the right path to God.

> "Some say the only right path is Islam and the rest stray or are on a deviant path. But I argue that there are many right paths. I try to justify a pluralistic view of religions— the internal sects of Sunni, Shia and others and also the great religions like Christianity, Judaism and the rest.

> "We think they go to hell and they think we go to hell," he added. "But I'm trying to say that Christians and members of other religions are well guided and good servants of God. All are equally rightful in what they believe.

> "To some, this sounds like heresy," he said, with a knowing smile and a small shrug. "But this too has found listening ears in our society."

barred from many types of employment and from inheriting property.

The Iranian government's treatment of the Baha'is is another indication of the intense importance given to religion and an example of how the government, in the name of protecting Islam, takes a central role in Iranians' lives.

Daily Life in the Islamic Republic

Under a government that is explicitly charged with promoting Islamic ideals, Iranians find that virtually every aspect of daily life is open to scrutiny for adherence to those ideals. From daily business transactions to what clothes men and women are allowed to wear in public to how men and women are allowed to interact, the government, through Islamic law, is present in the daily lives of the people.

Even the most intimate aspects of family life are subject to some form of governmental control. Iran has experienced a population explosion since the 1979 Islamic Revolution, when Iran's clerics proposed an anticontraception policy that encouraged a high birthrate. According to author Sandra Mackey, "The assumption of the revolutionaries in charge of government was that large numbers of Iranians would help the Islamic Republic propagate its ideology."[22] Within twenty years of the revolution, the population of Iran had nearly doubled, expanding from 34 million in 1979 to around 66 million in 2000. Eventually, the consequences of such dramatic population growth forced the authorities to reverse course, and a family-planning campaign launched by Iran's Health Ministry in the late 1980s has drastically reduced the country's population growth rate.

Education

As a result of Iran's two-decade-long population boom, today approximately half of its population is below the age of twenty-five. With so many young people, schooling is a high priority for Iranians. Government-run schools are free, and as a result 95 percent of Iranian children are able to attend primary or secondary schools. Although only five years of

An Iranian woman walks with her children. Approximately half the population of Iran is under the age of twenty-five.

primary education are compulsory, the literacy rate is high: About 77 percent of Iran's population can read and write. Author Ana Briongos explains the importance of education in Iran's society:

> Since the tenth century, education in Iran has been linked to religion. The Quran attributes a fundamental importance to learning and wisdom, with almost seven hundred and fifty versicles [verses] concerning education, reflection, knowledge or observation, but fewer than two hundred and fifty about law and the organisation of society. . . . The Quran and Hadith [the collective body of traditions relating to Muhammad] extol intellectual honesty and stress the obligation for all Muslims, men and women, to engage in the search for knowledge from the cradle to the grave, and to provide their children with an extensive, up-to-date education, drawing on new sources of knowledge wherever they are to be found, which may mean travelling, sometimes

to distant countries. Similarly, the Quran enjoins its readers to share skills and knowledge, not to hoard them, and above all not to use them for material gains, since society should be the sole beneficiary of learning.[23]

Iranian children begin school at age six or seven. Five years of elementary education is followed by three years of middle school and four years of high school. Iranian high schools offer three types of programs: general academic, a science and mathematics curriculum, and vocational and technical training. Regardless of whatever else they may choose to study, all students are required to study the Qur'an and the elements of Shia Islam.

This link between education and religion applies to higher education as well. Competition for higher education is tough, and only the brightest students can get in to state universities.

JOOBS

Author Maria O'Shea explains in her book *Iran: A Guide to Customs and Etiquette* (part of the Culture Shock! series) that in many Iranian cities and villages, water is distributed in open canals called *joobs*.

Throughout Iranian cities and towns you will see channels of water, or *joobs*, running alongside streets. Before tap water was supplied, these were the main water supplies for the population. They may originate in *qanats* or springs, and the supply could be diverted into individual houses, to fill their courtyard pools. The water was used for drinking, washing and waste disposal, so the nearer one lived to the supply the better. This explains why the north side of Tehran—the side nearest to the mountain water supply—has always been more desirable than the south. The same pattern of residence desirability is repeated in most Iranian towns and villages. In northern Tehran, the *joobs* provide a refreshing coolness on the main streets during summer, as well as water to wash the streets. In the poorer areas of south Tehran, the water is still used for domestic purposes, if not often for drinking. In the countryside, where there are no natural streams, the *joobs* flow to various parcels of land at set times, as the water is shared between those who maintain its supply.

Iranian boys study in a classroom. Ninety-five percent of Iranian children are able to attend school.

But cleverness alone is not enough to be accepted at one of the two hundred universities and colleges in Iran. The nation's Islamic ideals also play a role in determining who will be admitted. After the 1979 revolution, a government council closed down all the nation's institutions of higher education and revamped their curricula and textbooks so that they were purged of Western influence and reflected Islamic ideals instead. The colleges and universities reopened in December 1982, and according to author Sandra Mackey, "students applying for admission gained acceptance through their knowledge of Islam and their attitudes toward the Islamic Revolution as much as by their academic skills."[24]

For those students who wish to become religious scholars, the country also has a number of *madrases,* or Islamic colleges, particularly in Qom. Qom is one of the holiest cities in Iran, and is where the Ayatollah Khomeini studied theology, philosophy, and law as a young man. The city attracts Shiite scholars and students from all over the Muslim world. Author Ana Briongos explains that *madrases* like those in Qom are not like typical universities around the world:

[In Qom,] there are no imposing university buildings—there isn't even a university. The teachers aren't employed by anyone. It's up to the students to choose the scholar with whom they want to study. If he accepts them, the students go to the place where he lives and dispenses his learning, in one of the city's many *madrases*, or schools of Islamic studies. If a teacher is mediocre, he won't get students; if the standard of his teaching lapses, his students will leave him. An Islamic master is recognized as such for his ability to win over an audience. It's the students who make the teacher and give him approval. More than a simple teacher, the master should be a guide, a model, an example to imitate in every aspect of life.[25]

MUSLIM HOLIDAYS AND OBSERVANCES

Just as the Islamic Republic follows the Qur'an in its emphasis on education, Iranians also observe many Muslim

The city of Qom, one of the holiest cities in Iran, attracts students and scholars from all over the Muslim world.

THE IRANIAN BARBIE

Religion even has an impact on children's toys in Iran, where conservatives tried banning the popular Western fashion doll Barbie. The ban failed to dampen Iranian girls' enthusiasm for Barbie dolls, so conservatives instead ordered production of an Islamic version of Barbie. The new doll, dressed in a chador, was renamed Sara. Ken was renamed Dara and became Sara's brother.

In her book *The Last Great Revolution: Turmoil and Transformation in Iran*, author Robin Wright quotes Majid Qaderi, the director of Iran's Institute for Intellectual Development of Children, who designed the Islamic dolls, on the reasons the original Barbie was not acceptable to the Iranian government:

> Barbie is like a Trojan horse. Inside, it carries its Western cultural influences, such as makeup and indecent clothes. Once it enters our society, it dumps these influences on our children. . . . Barbie is an American woman who never wants to get pregnant and have babies. She never wants to look old and this contradicts our culture. Sara and Dara will reflect Islamic society.

religious holidays. The most extensive observance is of the *sawm* or fast during the month of Ramadan. Nothing is consumed between dawn and dusk during each day of Ramadan as a way of reminding worshipers of their dependence on God and of the hunger of the poor. At the end of Ramadan, there is a feast lasting three days known as Eid-e Fetr.

The Ramadan fast, Eid-e Fetr, and a few other holidays are observed by all Muslims, but some holidays are observed only by Shiites. For example, a celebration for all Muslims is the anniversary of the birth of Muhammad, but only Shiites celebrate certain other holidays, such as the birthday of Imam Ali.

While some holidays are celebrations, others are festivals of mourning. The most important festival of mourning for Shiite Muslims is Ashura, observed on the tenth day of the Islamic month of Moharram. Ashura is the anniversary of the martyrdom of Imam Hussein, who was killed in the Battle of Karbala in 680. Months before Ashura, individuals and groups all over Iran begin preparations for the passion plays and processions that will be central parts of the observance. According to journalists John Simpson and Tira Shubart, the Ashura observances begin early in the month of Moharram:

> During the ten days leading up to Ashura, the main procession day, groups called *hay'ats*, organised by local mosques or bazaar merchants, meet for a series of ritual dinners. These are charitable affairs, providing meals for the less fortunate, and each *hay'at* tries to outdo the others in generosity. In Tehran, hundreds of thousands of meals are given away. Over the years the significance of the *hay'ats* has grown; they are not only religious and cultural groups, but political ones as well. For many urban working-class people they represent the only non-governmental religious organisation open to them, and the regime has no control over it. During the last years of the Shah, it was the local *hay'ats* which smuggled in the audio cassettes of Khomeini's lectures in exile, and played them to neighbourhood groups. The SAVAK [secret police] found it very hard to infiltrate the *hay'ats*. When Ayatollah Khomeini finally returned

Men kneel in observance of Ashura, the Shiite Muslim festival of mourning.

to Iran, the *taaziyeh* [passion plays] and *Ashura* processions were celebrated with an extraordinary intensity: the down-trodden Shi'i had triumphed at last. And over the years that followed, the influence and the independence of the *hay'ats* did not diminish.[26]

The Ashura observance is an opportunity for Muslims to express both their grief over the martyrdom of Imam Hussein and their determination to fight injustice. The *taaziyeh* are an opportunity for ordinary Iranians to portray the major characters involved in the Battle of Karbala, and they may go to considerable lengths in reenacting this event. Some of the plays even include cavalry charges using local farm horses; their vividness brings the story of the martyrdom of Imam Hussein to life for the participants and observers. Then on Ashura itself, huge processions wind through the streets of major cities with hundreds of men expressing their grief by lashing themselves with chains, often causing bloody wounds. Although the government disapproves of these extreme expressions, attempts to curb them have proved futile.

No Ruz

As central as Islam is in daily life for the people of Iran, one of the most important Iranian holidays is not Islamic. No Ruz, the twelve-day-long celebration of the Persian New Year, is a festive holiday and an occasion for huge family celebrations. No Ruz, which literally means "New Day," occurs at the time of the vernal equinox, around March 21. The holiday comes from the Zoroastrian religion, which was dominant in pre-Islamic Iran. The festival includes lighting small bonfires symbolizing the sun. People jump over them, saying, "May your red radiance come to me. May my yellow tiredness go to you."[27]

Part of the No Ruz celebration is for the family to gather around a specially laid dinner table. On the table are seven items beginning with the Farsi letter *s*, such as apples (*sib*), garlic (*sir*), vinegar (*serkeh*), and seeds (*sabzi*). Also on the table are a copy of the Qur'an, a bowl of goldfish to symbolize life, a mirror to reflect evil, and colored eggs. Author Ana Briongos explains the significance of the eggs:

> The mother is supposed to eat as many hard-boiled eggs as she has children, and even those mothers who

never eat eggs do their best, to everyone's amusement. The eggs are placed in front of the mirror that adorns the No Ruz table. According to an old legend, the eggs move when the year changes, because the earth rests on the horn of a mythological bull (who lives in turn on the back of a huge whale in the sea) and after carrying it for a year on one horn, the bull gets tired and has to shift it across to the other.[28]

Because the origins of No Ruz are Persian rather than Islamic, government officials have expressed disapproval of its ancient festivities and branded them superstitious and anti-Islamic. And according to Briongos, "It is rumoured that the mullahs want to eliminate the festival, by bringing it forward to coincide with the anniversary of the Revolution."[29] But despite the official disapproval, No Ruz celebrations flourish in homes all over Iran.

PUBLIC AND PRIVATE SPACE

One reason No Ruz celebrations flourish despite official disapproval is that the right to privacy is held in high regard in Iran. The Iranian belief in the right to privacy is expressed in many ways. For example, Iranians make a distinction between what is public and what is private in their homes. Certain behaviors that would be condemned in public—such as a woman going bareheaded—are acceptable in one's own home or the homes

Iranian women wear Western-style clothing at a private party. Behavior that would be condemned in public is considered acceptable in the privacy of one's home.

of others. Part of the reason for this is that "inside" and "outside" are strictly differentiated in Iran. For his book *The Mantle of the Prophet*, author Roy Mottahedeh interviewed an Iranian man who wished to remain anonymous but whom the author refers to as Ali Hashemi. Mottahedeh describes the division between "inside" and "outside" in Ali's home:

> The rest of the doors led to the two principal sections of the house, called in Persian the *andaruni*, "the in-

 ## A MOURNING CEREMONY IN DEH KOH

The book *Women of Deh Koh: Lives in an Iranian Village*, by Erika Friedl, describes various aspects of life for the women of this village in Iran, the name of which the author has fictionalized. In the following passage, Friedl describes the mourning ceremony for one of the village women, in which the men and women mourned separately, in accord with the Islamic customs of Iran.

> Begom's long-suffering sister finally had died. Although she came from only a small family and had been old and sick for quite some time, as the widow and mother of successful and well-regarded men she was mourned in style by her people. In small groups of neighbors and relatives, half the village was flowing in and out of the mourning sessions in Begom's sister's house, men and women separately. For three days, from morning until deep into the night, the porch and living room were crowded with dark-clad women and little children sitting on rugs along the walls, drinking tea, talking in hushed tones, and sobbing in refrain to the songs one or another of the women would sing in a shrill falsetto, veil drawn across half her face. From time to time also Begom or one of the dead woman's other sisters or one of her daughters would work herself up into a frenzy of grief and throw herself into the circle of squatting women, wailing loudly, writhing in the pain of loss, and bemoaning, in a sob-choked sing-song, her own great sorrow, the dead woman's virtues, her last days, the moments of her death. The performance over, she would collect herself and then go back to brewing more tea or directing the preparation of meals for those mourners who had come a long way.

side," and the *biruni*, "the outside." As a small child Ali
seldom visited the biruni, which was exclusively for his
father and his father's male guests, but when he did, he
was always struck by its resemblance to the "inside."
Not only was the house divided into two but everything
inside the *andaruni* and *biruni* was divided into twos.
Each of the two sections was built around a garden, and
each garden was clearly divided into two. As you en-
tered there was a right-hand side and a left-hand side,
each mirroring the other: if there was a cypress planted
near the end of the right-hand side, there was sure to be
a cypress at the end of the left-hand side as well. There
were two long rooms on each side of the *biruni*, and at
the end were two small rooms, all of them two steps
above the level of the garden. . . .

The total isolation of the more public "outside" from the
"inside" part of the house was one rule of division in
two that no one dared violate. There was no opening,
not even a window, that joined the *andaruni* and the
biruni.[30]

This sanctity of private space has a long history in Iran and
is rooted in the early days of Islam. The Qur'an teaches:

O you who believe, let your dependants and those

who have not yet reached the age of puberty,

ask permission (to enter your presence) on three
    occasions:

Before the early morning prayer;

When you disrobe for the mid-day siesta;

And after prayer at night.

These are the three occasions of [privacy] for you.

There is no harm if you or they visit one another

at other times (without permission).

God thus explains things to you clearly,

for God is all-knowing and all-wise.

When your children have reached the age of puberty,

they should similarly ask your leave (for entering)

as others did before them.

God thus clearly explains his commands to you,

for God is all-knowing and all-wise.[31]

The strict laws that require women to be covered in public do not apply to private property. For example, Shahrzad Hajmoshir is a divorced woman who lives in north Tehran. Hajmoshir walks outside on her own land bareheaded. "This is my property, my space," she explained to author Elaine Sciolino. "No one from the outside has the right to invade it or look at me."[32]

The respect for privacy also means that when Iranians gather for a meal in a private home, they can discuss topics that would be taboo in public. Wright describes what a meal for Iranians in a private home is like:

Iranians share a meal in a private home.

> Over a typical meal of grilled lamb or chicken and saffron rice, goat cheese, flat bread and onions, they love to discuss and feistily debate. Some subjects—such as atheism—are

best avoided, at least at first. Yet politics, religion, women's rights, money and even sex, including birth control, can be dinner table conversation. Curiosity and candor are two strong Iranian traits. They'll probe virtually any subject— and in the privacy of their homes, the revolution has not kept them from doing so.[33]

KETMAN AND TAAROF

Although Iranians may discuss sensitive subjects in their own homes, they also place a high value on the sanctity of their private thoughts. People who keep their thoughts to themselves are regarded as wise and mature. Iranians see this practice, called *ketman*, as a way to guard the dignity of other people. But according to writer Ana Briongos, who has traveled extensively in Iran, you can never be sure

> whether people are telling you what they *really* think, be- cause they have a thoroughly theatrical attitude to life. They are always on stage, always acting, and are trained to do so from a tender age. This training has been handed down for centuries and is very much a part of Iranian life. It's a stratagem for protecting private thoughts and feel- ings, and has come to be a permanent institution, with a name of its own: it is known as *ketman*.[34]

In addition to *ketman*, Iranian etiquette includes the cus- tom of *taarof*—saying something to be polite. Iranians often use flattery or false modesty to maintain the harmony of so- cial situations. *Taarof* also includes generous, even exagger- ated, offers of hospitality, such as inviting houseguests to stay indefinitely but expecting them to leave in a day or two. Iranians seem to understand and accept this custom of ex- aggerated politeness, but Westerners can find it confusing, frustrating, and even dishonest. According to Sciolino,

> Even my most trusted friends in Iran are accomplished in what I consider the art of lying. Over tea at a diplo- mat's house one afternoon, an American woman who had recently arrived in Iran modeled a full black robe and headdress that had been custom-made for her in Egypt. The headdress covered every strand of hair and part of her forehead; the sleeves came long and tight over her wrists. It was overkill. It told the authorities,

"Not only do I accept your restrictions about women's dress, I revel in them." Nazila [an Iranian friend of Sciolino's] told her that it was lovely. "Maybe I should have one made for myself," she added.

"Why would you ever wear something like that?" I asked Nazila after the encounter.

"I wouldn't," she said.

"Then why did you make such a fuss about it?"

"It's *taarof*," Nazila explained. "It's exaggerated good manners that keep the peace. My mother always tells me I have bad manners because I usually don't do *taarof*. But in this case, I felt I had no choice. No harm was done."

Taarof is reflected in everyday Persian expressions of excessive politeness that when translated literally diminish the self in front of others: "I sacrifice myself for you." "I am your slave maiden." "Step on my eyes."[35]

INDUSTRY COMES HOME

Because women face many restrictions when they are outside their homes, one traditional industry, carpet weaving, is still carried out in many private homes. Earning $2 billion a year, the carpet trade employs a large number of people in villages all over the country, including such renowned carpet-weaving centers as Ardestan, Esfahan, and Shiraz. According to Briongos, most women in Iran, except in Tehran, contribute to the family income by weaving carpets. She describes the carpet-weaving industry in the private homes of Ardestan:

> You might imagine that behind these walls there are well-guarded harems, enveloped in veils and sumptuous cloths. But no, behind these walls there are normal families. In each village, they opened their doors and offered us tea, shade and company. The most secret thing behind the walls was the skill in the hands of the women knotting fine carpets; the most colourful, the balls of wool they were using.[36]

Carpet weaving is often a family business. The women do the actual weaving, but are assisted in many ways by their

An Iranian woman at work weaving a carpet.

children. In a small desert village named Khvor, where the average income is less than $150 a month, most girls leave school after fifth grade in order to participate in the family business of carpet weaving. These handmade carpets usually earn between $300 and $1,000 each, and the extra money helps families make ends meet. One man who lives near the Caspian Sea and earns $100 a month working as a security guard supplements his income by raising silkworms in one room of his house. The cocoons of the silkworms produce fibers that are used for weaving carpets and making textiles.

Men generally are in charge of getting the carpets to the bazaars for sale. In the larger cities, the bazaars may have dozens of shops where carpets are sold both to Iranians and to visitors from around the world. Carpet weaving is Iran's second largest industry; only oil brings in more revenue.

EMPLOYMENT IN IRAN

Although the oil industry is the most economically productive sector of the Iranian economy—Iran is the third largest oil exporter in the world—it is not the nation's biggest employer. Relatively few workers are needed to operate the wells, refineries, and shipping facilities that keep oil flowing. Iran also manufactures chemicals, grows a substantial portion of the world's pistachios, and produces caviar from Caspian Sea sturgeon. The Persian Gulf region is important both for trade with other countries and for industries such as fishing, pearl diving, sailcloth and reed mat making, and camel breeding.

The majority of Iranians—approximately three-fourths—work in the private sector, while around one-fifth work in the public sector. The average salary in Iran is only around $1,600 a year. According to a report issued in 2001 by the Public Relations Office of the Statistics Center of Iran, official unemployment was 14.3 percent nationwide, but some experts say the figure is closer to 20 percent.

Many Iranians have found various ways to cope with low pay or unemployment. One young man in Tehran made photocopies of a job application form he found in a magazine and sold the copies on a street corner for five cents apiece. Tehran and other large cities in Iran also have a booming unofficial taxi business. Many citizens illegally use their private cars as taxis. These unregistered taxis carry five or more passengers at a time. Another form of illegal employment is called junk theft—rummaging through residential trash bins for recyclable items such as plastic, which is then illegally sold to recycling factories. Many of these junk thieves are homeless people who are arrested and beaten if they are caught. According to an article on the Iran Mania website, "Garbage collectors from [Tehran] frequently clash with the 'junk thieves' who search the trash cans when they are put out for emptying after sunset."[37]

WOMEN IN IRANIAN SOCIETY

Whatever work they do, and despite Islamic restrictions on public behavior, men and women often work side by side in Iran. Women participate in Iranian society in most of the ways women do in the West. For example, 4 percent of the Majlis is female, and women also serve in administrative jobs in the government and in the professions. But there are also differences, the most obvious of which is *hejab*, or modest dress. In Iran, men must wear long trousers and long-

sleeved shirts, and women are required to have their bodies
covered except for the hands and face. It is particularly important for the hair to be covered, either with a traditional
one-piece garment called a chador or a more Western-style
overcoat known as a manteau. Modesty regulations also include separating men and women from each other in many
settings, but this is often impossible because women are active in so many areas of public life. The result is a complex
and confusing set of practices. According to Sciolino,

> The existence of the *hejab* is apparently not enough to
> separate men and women, and male-female relation-
> ships work themselves out in public spaces in irrational
> ways. There is no clear-cut definition of a sexually inte-
> grated public space. Women may be segregated from
> men in government offices, but are squeezed close to
> them in the buildings' overburdened elevators. Men and

TESTING THE LIMITS OF *HEJAB*

Hejab is the term for modest dress, which includes mandatory veiling of women in Iran. In her book *Persian Mirrors: The Elusive Face of Iran*, journalist Elaine
Sciolino discusses this controversial issue.

I have often asked women friends what would happen if
on International Women's Day every woman opposed to
compulsory veiling marched bareheaded in the name of
choice. Some women say it wouldn't be a big deal because
most Iranian women in Iran would choose to keep on
their scarves and chadors—either out of choice or out of
fear. Some women say they have bigger battles to fight,
such as equal rights in matters of employment, divorce,
inheritance, and child custody. Some say they have even
learned to have fun with the *hejab*, constantly testing the
limits. Others say that there would be no safety in numbers. They predict that women would be arrested, beaten,
even killed en masse. Sometimes I think that the era of the
forced head covering has passed, but that no one really
knows how to deal with it. It seems that even those in
power know that the policy of forcing women to wear *hejab* has not created believers. If anything, it has added to
cynicism and the questioning of Islam itself.

women are required to use separate entrances at airports, but they sit next to each other on domestic flights.[38]

According to Islamic regulations, touching a woman to whom a man is not related is unacceptable, and so men and women in Iran do not shake hands when they meet. On city buses, men and women sit in separate sections. Even men and women who are married to each other are not allowed to sit together—men sit at the front and women sit at the back. However, on buses traveling between cities, couples and families are allowed to sit together.

Iranian society is sexually segregated both by custom and by law. For example, men and women have to stand in separate lines to buy bread. And in 1999, Iran's parliament passed a law decreeing that women must go to female doctors and men must go to male doctors. But in Tehran, an exception to the rules about the separation of men and women is taxis, which generally will take as many passengers as can wedge themselves in, men and women. Of course, the women must wear Islamic dress, but they often sit in very cramped conditions with men, and this is accepted as normal. And according to Sciolino, "Men and women can sit so

Iranian schoolgirls pose for the camera. Strict dress codes force women and girls to be completely covered in public, even in hot summer weather.

HEJAB IN THE SUMMER

Alison Wearing, a Canadian, visited Iran in the late 1990s with a male companion named Ian. In her book *Honeymoon in Purdah*, Wearing describes what it was like to wear the clothing prescribed for women in Iran while traveling during the summer.

On a bus. Where we have been for the last five hours and where we'll be for three more to come. It was desert when we started, and it is certainly desert for as far as the heat ripples will allow us to see. The only thing I am interested in doing is trying to figure out whether it is possible that I am urinating through my skin, as I haven't peed in three days. With remarkably little condescension, Ian assures me this is unlikely. I decide to try to take my mind off it, think about something else, so I concentrate instead on which moves faster: the sweat trickling down my arms into the palms of my hands or the sweat trickling down my legs into the soles of my shoes. Or the sweat trickling down my face and swan-diving from my chin onto my lap.

Ian, dear Ian, is not sweating at all. His nose is ever so slightly moist at the tip and, with the sleeves of his light cotton shirt rolled up, his arms are as dry as the wind. His skin runs a deep tan after all these weeks in the desert. He is talking and laughing with several people on the bus and looks so carefree and good-natured at the moment that I think I hate him.

Today, as every day, I am wearing black leather shoes, black socks, white cotton underwear with blue flowers and a tiny girly bow on the waistband, green cotton trousers, a white bra with some lacy bits that make my chest feel like a screened-in porch and metal clasps that sink into my skin like staples, a long-sleeved cotton shirt, a floor-length black polyester coat, and a black polyester scarf folded down over my forehead, back across my ears and clipped under my chin. It was 43 degrees Celsius [109 degrees Fahrenheit] when we got onto the bus. But it's a dry heat, as Ian pointed out this morning, so you see, you can barely feel it.

tightly packed in taxis that there is a popular expression for going on a date: going for a taxi ride."[39] In other cities, however, unrelated men and women sometimes go through an elaborate dance to avoid sitting next to one another. Author Alison Wearing describes a taxi ride in a city on the Caspian coast in which she had to get out of the cab three times in three blocks to avoid sitting next to male passengers.

IRAN'S YOUNG PEOPLE

In a country where contact between males and females is so strictly regulated, it is often difficult for members of the opposite sex to meet and get acquainted. Young people are chaperoned, which means that in any situation involving social contact with non–family members of the opposite sex, there is close supervision, usually by an older family member. In addition, many marriages are arranged through family ties. The experience of Javad and Tahereh, an Iranian couple, is typical:

> The . . . couple's marriage had been arranged when a mutual friend introduced their parents. After the parents had agreed to a potential match, Javad was allowed to call on Tahereh and chat—once. A week later, Tahereh had received a marriage proposal from Javad relayed from his parents to her aunt and to her. Her acceptance went back along the same route. The next time they met was to come to the [family-planning] clinic, with chaperones.[40]

Iranians have few opportunities to meet members of the opposite sex without a chaperone. This is a difficult situation for many young people. There is a ban on public dating and even on hand-holding in public, and boys and girls are not supposed to socialize openly with each other. Many Iranians have found ways to defy the restrictions placed on their social lives. According to author Robin Wright,

> As the 1990s progressed, Tehran was rife with tales of forbidden youthful encounters across the gender barrier. Males and females walked together in parks. They planned picnics in "separate" groups of males and females on blankets positioned just a bit apart. They hung out in malls where the boys might brush by the girls and ask for a telephone number or suggest a meeting somewhere else. They crossed paths at Tehran's new Cyber Café, where the young flocked to surf the Internet and send e-mail over complimentary coffee—albeit on separate floors for the separate sexes.

Young Iranians proved ingenious in their efforts to socialize. One of dozens of tales I heard over the years in-

volved Basij [members of a military group] stopping eight kids on the ski slopes reserved for females in the Alborz Mountains. All were covered in the required head covers and body drapes, but facial stubble had given four of them away. Desperate to be with the girls, the boys had donned Islamic dress as a disguise.[41]

Iranian teens assemble in a secluded location. Iranian law forbids boys and girls from socializing with each other in public.

Young people who are caught breaking the law may face harsh penalties, including arrest and lashing. This was a major issue in 2001, as Revolutionary Guards, who are controlled by conservative clerics, stepped up their enforcement of the public morality laws. For many people, young and old, the conservatives' interpretation of Islam is no longer acceptable to them, and they are searching for new solutions.

5 Art and Culture

Like most aspects of life in Iran, the arts reflect the blending of the nation's Persian and Islamic heritages as well as other influences. Some Iranian artists work in traditional media using traditional themes and techniques. Others are much more modern in their approach and push the limits of what is acceptable under the restrictions imposed by the Islamic Republic.

PERSIAN POTTERY

Pottery is one of Iran's oldest art forms and clearly displays a blend of Persian and Islamic influences. In the first millennium A.D., pottery was painted with characteristic Persian designs, such as geometric, floral, and animal motifs. The lotus flower, a symbol of life and women, was a frequent Persian design in the years before the Arab conquest.

By the ninth century, Islamic influences were incorporated with Persian traditions in the designs, and Persian pottery had become famous well beyond the nation's borders. The nomads of northeastern Iran had developed their own method of glazing and were adding Islamic elements to the decoration of their pottery such as *Kufic* script, the style of Arabic lettering used in the first written versions of the Qur'an. When a more durable type of clay began to be used in the thirteenth century, demand for Persian pottery grew even larger as people found it was both beautiful and practical. Brilliant colors began to be used, and even today pottery from Tabriz is known for its distinctive shade of turquoise.

With the coming of the industrial age and the introduction of mass-produced metal and glass utensils in the nineteenth century, the use of Persian pottery in homes began to decline, and production of pottery declined as well. In recent years, though, Iran has been promoting a revival in pottery making. For example, a ceramic exhibition opened in Tabriz in August 2001. There, according to the official in charge of the art gallery, "Some 274 works from 90 artists are on display at the ongoing exhibition."[42]

Contemporary Iranian pottery looks much like it has for the past two thousand years. At a recent exhibition of contemporary pottery in Tehran, there were jugs, bowls, vessels, and vases in shapes that would have been recognizable in ancient Persia. There were also some more modern-looking

A plate from thirteenth-century Persia.

pieces such as a vase in the shape of a pomegranate, a glazed black stoneware teapot, and decorative pieces in animal shapes such as an owl, a cow, and a fish.

The representation of living creatures is generally forbidden in Sunni Islam as a way to avoid even the possibility of idol worship. In Iran, however, which follows the Shia branch of Islam, images of humans and animals are common in works of art, though not allowed on religious buildings. Works of art that depict living creatures include handmade pottery, such as that on display at Tabriz, and Iran's world-renowned Persian carpets.

PERSIAN CARPETS

Persian carpets, perhaps the best-known cultural export from Iran, are another example of the blending of Persian

Persian carpets like this one are handwoven out of wool, cotton, or silk. Carpets from the pre-Islamic era contain geometric and floral designs.

and Islamic influences in the arts. Carpets made before the Islamic era usually featured balanced designs with geometric and floral patterns in rectangular plots that represented the ideal Persian garden. Designs featuring animals and humans were also popular. After the Arab conquest, Islamic motifs such as verses of the Qur'an were woven into carpets, combined with classic Persian designs.

Modern Persian carpets and rugs still incorporate religious symbols, but weavers today also draw inspiration for their designs from their everyday surroundings, such as animals, trees, and flowers. As with pottery, the lotus flower is a particularly popular design.

Persian carpets are handwoven out of wool, cotton, or silk. Everyday rugs are most commonly made of wool, while decorative rugs often contain silk, which is less durable than wool. Higher-quality rugs have more knots per square inch—up to fifty. Rugs designed for everyday use may have thirty to forty knots per square inch.

PERSIAN ARCHITECTURE

As popular as Persian rugs are, the distinctly Persian style of Islamic architecture that emerged in Iran is regarded by some as the country's greatest contribution to world culture. Since the first centuries of the Islamic era, Persian architecture has greatly influenced the design of buildings in other Islamic countries, especially Pakistan, Afghanistan, and India.

Persian architecture is very simple in structure and design, but intricate surface ornamentation and bold colors make it appear more complex than it is. Buildings constructed before the Islamic era typically have a courtyard and covered arcades, rectangular entrance porticoes, and *iwans*, which are vaulted hallways that lead to the courtyard. Another characteristically Persian feature is the dome, which Persian architects pioneered during the Sassanian period (A.D. 224–637). Domes are either conical or onion shaped and rest on square chambers by using two intermediate levels known as squinches to support the dome. The lower squinch is octagonal, and the higher squinch is sixteen sided.

The Arab conquest of Iran in the mid–seventh century introduced Islamic elements to Persian architecture. These features included high pointed arches, arches within arches,

The Imam Khomeni Mosque in central Iran. Iranian builders incorporated traditional Persian features such as domes and arches into mosque designs.

domes within domes, and pairs of minarets, which are tall towers from which the faithful are called to prayer. The mosque, rather than the enormous palaces built by Persian rulers, became the major building type. Iranians added characteristically Persian features such as the *iwan* and dome to the traditional Islamic mosque design. The typical Persian mosque has a large courtyard accessed by *iwans* and surrounded by arched cloisters, or covered passageways. The *mehrab*, a niche that indicates the direction of Mecca, is located behind the cloisters.

The Arab conquest changed not only the dominant type of buildings but also the type of decoration that was allowed. Persians had long decorated their buildings with colorful frescoes and patterns of mosaics, but the Islamic restriction on the representation of human forms on religious buildings meant that ornamentation on mosques had to be geometric,

ESFAHAN'S MASJED-E EMAM

One of the high points in the history of Persian architecture occurred during the Safavid dynasty (1501–1722). Some of the most notable mosques and palaces built during that period are located at Esfahan, which was the Safavid capital. The centerpiece of the city is Emam Khomeini Square. (Before the Islamic Revolution it was known as Shah Jahan Square.)

Emam Khomeini Square measures over sixteen hundred by five hundred feet and contains several beautiful and historic buildings, including what is probably the most magnificent mosque in Iran, the Masjed-e Emam. Construction on the mosque began in 1611 under the reign of Shah Abbas I and continued for eighteen years. The entrance portal is meant to complement the entrance to the Bozorg Bazaar at the other end of the square. It is constructed of a foundation of white marble from the Persian province of Ardestan, topped by an arch decorated with elaborate floral, geometric, and calligraphic designs. Although the portal looks symmetrical to casual observers, the architect actually designed in slight irregularities; to build anything without error was thought to be an attempt to imitate the perfection of God.

Inside the portal, the mosque itself is angled to face toward Mecca, the direction in which Muslims pray. The inner courtyard of the mosque contains a pool for the ablutions Muslims perform before prayer and is surrounded by mosaics dominated by unusually intense shades of blue and yellow. The main sanctuary has a double dome. The interior dome rises 120 feet above the floor, while the top of the outer dome is nearly 170 feet high. The ceiling is decorated in a golden rose pattern surrounded by elaborate circular mosaics set against a blue background. Visitors are often seen sitting in quiet corners of the mosque gazing up in awe at the beauty of the building and its decorations.

Once completed, the mosque and its associated theological school were supervised by the shah's father-in-law, Sheikh Lotofallah, an Islamic scholar from Lebanon, for whom another of the square's mosques is now named.

Construction of the Masjed-e Emam (pictured) began in 1611 during the reign of Shah Abbas I.

floral, and calligraphic designs. Walls may contain mosaics forming the word *Allah* or *Muhammad* repeated hundreds of times in the highly stylized *Kufic* script. The surfaces of mosques, domes, and minarets are covered with ceramic tiles in blue, green, yellow, and red that form intricate patterns. Verses from the Qur'an are also a common ornamentation on religious buildings. Other structures, such as government buildings, are often inscribed with verses from Iran's great poets.

PERSIAN POETRY

Poetry has been one of the most important forms of creative expression in Iran throughout history. Iranians continue to admire their great poets, and Iran's classical poetry has remained part of the consciousness of the Iranian people. One of the most famous Persian poets was Muhammad Shams od-Din Hafez, who lived during the fourteenth century. The Ayatollah Khomeini was greatly influenced by Hafez and wrote poetry himself.

Poetry can serve as a source of information about ancient Persia. The vast poem known as the *Shaname,* or Book of Kings, is the repository of the central myths, legends, and history of the Persian empires up until the death of Yazdegerd III in A.D. 652. No one knows exactly when the stories in the *Shaname* began to be composed or collected, but some of them also appear in the Zoroastrian holy book, the Zend Avesta, which was written around 500 B.C. Several Persian kings commissioned poets to bring the stories together into a single narrative, but the most successful attempt, and the one that most people refer to when they speak of the *Shaname,* was the one done by Abdul Qasim Ferdowsi, who was born in approximately 940.

When Ferdowsi began working on it, the *Shaname* had been neglected for about two hundred years. Ferdowsi saw himself as the savior of the *Shaname.* He wrote in Farsi, the native language of Persia, and he is recognized today as a brilliant poet and as a preserver of Persian language, history, and culture. Ferdowsi spent thirty-five years transforming the diverse stories of the *Shaname* tradition into a connected narrative poem of fifty thousand couplets. According to scholar and translator Jerome W. Clinton,

The *Shaname* has had a sustained and vital influence within its cultural tradition comparable to that of the Old Testament or Homer's works within theirs. It depicts the beliefs and values of Iranian society as they were before the coming of Islam, and so has helped to mark them as distinctive with the complex mix of elements that make up Islamic culture. Its heroes embody ideals of personal conduct that are still current, and its vision of Iranian society as one that is sustained by a divinely sanctioned monarchy pervades the whole course of Iranian history.[43]

Perhaps the best-known Iranian poet in the West is Omar Khayyam, who was born in 1048. (In Iran, Omar Khayyam is also known for his work as a mathematician, historian, and astronomer.) Many of his works of poetry, including the famous *Rubaiyat*, were translated into English in the mid–nineteenth century by the poet Edward FitzGerald.

Even though the greatest Persian poets lived centuries ago, poetry still plays a central part in the lives of Iranians. Iranians use phrases from poets such as Hafez, Sa'di, and

Tomb of the tenth-century Persian poet Abdul Qasim Ferdowsi.

others in everyday conversation, and they love to get together for poetry readings. Writer Ana Briongos describes one of her experiences illustrating the importance of poetry in Iran:

> Before bed Bahram and his mother recite poetry for us, hand in hand. Quite amazing. Some relatives and neighbours drop by, as they do each day, and join in the recital. All Iranians know lots of poems, by Hafez, Sa'di, [Ferdowsi] . . . and they like to recite them when they get together. One starts off, then another takes over, and it's a moving experience for everybody. Bahram's mother brings over the thick volume of Hafez's poems and gives it to me to open at any page. The poem will reveal my destiny. They read it aloud. The poem says I will share the aroma of wine and the scent of Golestani roses with the poor and the footloose, and that my heart's thirst for foreign lands will never be quenched. For me it's a moment of glory. Then the book changes hands, and the ceremony continues. Wherever in the world two Iranians meet, chances are they will end up hand in hand reciting poetry. Bricklayers at work don't sing, they recite poems by Omar Khayyam. In Iran, poetry has always been the way to resist oppression; its coded language fosters wordplay, and helps lovers, members of the underground and everyone, in the end, to sublimate aspirations that can't be realised in this wretched world.[44]

Iran continues to produce poets, but they must deal with the strict censorship placed on them by the government. Anything critical of Islam or the current regime is not allowed. Many poets fled the country in the early 1980s to avoid arrest or persecution and to gain artistic freedom.

IRANIAN CINEMA

Although it is common for Iranians to enjoy poetry, movies are one of the most popular forms of entertainment in Iran, and the country boasts an active film industry. Dozens of Iranian films are released each year, and they are an important part of the country's popular culture. As Peter Chelkowski and Hamid Dabashi, who wrote the book *Staging a Revolution: The Art of Persuasion in the Islamic Republic of Iran*, explain,

THE DAY I BECAME A WOMAN

Despite the strict censorship of films in the Islamic Republic, Iranian filmmakers constantly push the limits of what is acceptable. One subject that has long been taboo in Iranian cinema is the status of women. However, the film *The Day I Became a Woman* deals critically with the role of women in Iranian society. The director of this feminist film was a woman named Marzieh Meshkini. She decided to make the film as a collection of three short films rather than a feature because short films are not required to have government script approval and production permits.

The title story is about a little girl named Hava who is told on her ninth birthday that, according to Islamic law, she is a woman now and must wear the chador, an ankle-length black veil. Hava cannot go outside and play with her friends anymore but must dress and behave as an adult. The second story follows a woman named Ahoo, who is one of a group of chador-clad women racing along the Persian Gulf Coast on bicycles. They are being pursued by a group of men on horseback, including Ahoo's husband, who commands her to come home. The third story shows an old woman who spends her large inheritance on household luxury items and then sets up housekeeping on the beach. The theme of each film focuses on the difficult situations faced by women as a result of Iran's restrictive laws and customs.

The Day I Became a Woman played in only one theater in Iran, where the poster of Ahoo riding on her bicycle was banned—bicycle riding is forbidden for women in Iran. According to the director, who was interviewed on National Public Radio's *Morning Edition* on April 16, 2001 (available at *www.npr.org*), "They have not allowed for the poster of my film to be posted on the top of that movie theater, and the only thing that now is there is just a black piece of cloth, on it written in red, 'The Day I Became a Woman.'"

Cinema has been by far the most popular form of entertainment in modern Iranian history. No other form of public entertainment comes even close to cinema in the range of its appeal in the popular culture. Traditional forms of public entertainment . . . gradually gave way to the fascination of the Iranian public with these moving pictures that talked and enchanted their way into the modern Iranian consciousness.[45]

As popular as they are, Iranian films still must comply with restrictive Islamic guidelines. In the mid-1990s, Iran's Ministry of Culture and Islamic Guidance issued censorship rules for cinema, television programs, and stage performances. These rules banned close-ups and makeup for women. Scenes of women running were also banned to prevent their movement from accentuating the shape of their bodies. And the sacred names of Muhammad, Ali, Hassan, and Hussein were not to be used for antagonists.

The Farabi Foundation is a state-sponsored agency that was established to supervise the production and distribution of feature films in Iran. Censors must approve the scripts of new movies before they begin production. They also review movies, both those produced in Iran and foreign films, before they are released to theaters. Any offensive scenes are either cut entirely or blacked out. Themes of adultery, prostitution, homosexuality, suicide, divorce, and domestic violence are not approved.

Occasionally, a film with banned material in it slips through the censorship system—but only briefly. One very controversial movie, *Taste of Cherry*, deals with the taboo subject of suicide. The movie concerned the censors because it showed sympathy for a man contemplating suicide rather than depicting his actions as sinful. The University of Tehran hosted the film's only showing in Iran.

Although films must conform to a strictly enforced interpretation of Islamic ideals and many contain elements showing support for the Islamic Revolution, most do not have overtly religious themes. Many movies produced in Iran today contain a great deal of action and violence, as titles such as *Play with Death* and *Escape from Hell* suggest. But films are also beginning to depict the down-to-earth daily life of Iranians, focusing on themes such as the lives of children, and several of these have won international acclaim. For example, the film *A Time for Drunken Horses*, which tells the story of an ill twelve-year-old boy and his family's efforts to raise enough money for an operation that will save his life, won three awards at the 2000 Cannes Film Festival.

Yet according to Sciolino, these films do not always portray everyday life accurately because the way relationships are depicted must conform to Iran's censorship rules. For example, in films, husbands and wives do not touch each other, and parents do not touch daughters older than nine or sons older than thirteen, Iran's legal age for marriage. However, filmmakers have found various ways to deal with the restrictions placed on them. Director Mojtaba Raie explains that "we can't show kissing or touching to say the characters love each other. We have to find an artistic way to show it—through behavior toward each other or through the forgiveness they show each other."[46] In many movies lovers are shown gazing longingly at each other instead of embracing.

The lengths to which filmmakers may go to work within the censors' restrictions can be extreme. One director got around the ban on depicting female actresses giving birth on-screen by dressing as a woman and playing the part himself. And although in reality women are allowed to wear whatever they want in private, even in scenes depicting home life, they must keep their hair and bodies covered on-screen. Writer Elaine Sciolino explains how one director dealt with the restrictions placed on his films: "The director Dariush Mehrjui made it seem more natural for his actresses to have their heads covered at home by putting the heroine of his 1990 film *Hamoun* in a bathrobe, a bath towel wrapped around her head, as if she had just emerged from the shower, or by showing a woman doing chores around the house with a scarf holding her hair in place."[47]

THE BAHMAN CULTURAL CENTER

Some Iranian films get their first showing at the Bahman Cultural Center for the Performing Arts in Tehran. The cultural center is named after the Persian month Bahman, during which the shah left Iran and Khomeini came back. It is a complex of several buildings and was created along with several other new centers in Tehran in the 1990s to provide entertainment such as cinema, plays, music, and art.

The Bahman Center has a theater where plays from Iran and other countries are performed. Plays performed there must conform to the same strict guidelines as films in Iran, including *hejab*: Women must have their hair covered and have no exposed skin other than their hands and faces,

OTHELLO IN WONDERLAND

Many Iranian writers who fled the country after the revolution continued to write in exile. Gholamhoseyn Sa'edi was a prominent writer of short stories, plays, and screenplays as well as a political activist. Because of his outspoken views on censorship and political oppression in Iran, he fled the country in the early 1980s. He lived in exile in Paris until his death in 1985. One of his best-known plays is *Othello in Wonderland*, which uses as its centerpiece Shakespeare's play *Othello*. Set in sixteenth-century Venice, Shakespeare's play tells how the title character, an African Muslim general hired by Venice, marries a Venetian woman named Desdemona and then is tricked into killing her by his jealous aide Iago. Sa'edi's play criticizes the revolutionary government's power to control the arts in Iran by portraying government agents as ignorant and inept. The article "Drama" by M.R. Ghanoonparvar (available at *www.iranian.com*) discusses Sa'edi's play.

> Sa'edi took advantage of the Islamic regime's stated support for the arts, particularly the theater, to create a farce about the production of Shakespeare's *Othello* in Persia, where it is transformed into a propaganda tool for the revolutionary government and its opposition to the superpowers. Under official supervision and watched by a revolutionary guard armed with a machine gun, the director and actors are forced to transform the character of Othello into a revolutionary fighter representing the downtrodden and Iago into a counterrevolutionary. Even Shakespeare, sometimes called Brother Shakespeare and confused by the official in charge with the character of Othello in the play, is thought to have been a Muslim who lived, anachronistically, in pre-Islamic times. The government agents also force the female actors to cover themselves from head to foot in full Islamic dress and even object to Othello's speaking affectionately to Desdemona.

and men must wear long trousers and long-sleeved shirts. Plays written by Iranians rarely present a difficulty in this regard, but plays imported from elsewhere are another matter. Ahmad Torabi, the aide to Bahman's managing director, explains: "There's less of a problem with women's parts if we do plays from a long time ago. We hope to do *Cat on a Hot Tin Roof* by . . . Tennessee Williams in the fall, with Islamic *hejab* of course and maybe some slight adaptations to the script."[48]

Even plays from much earlier times can present problems, however. Russian playwright Anton Chekhov's play *The Bear* has been performed at Bahman. The play was written in 1888, and the costume of the female lead was deemed acceptably modest by Islamic authorities, but the script still had to be edited, as author Robin Wright explains. "The romantic interplay between the widow and a neighboring landowner was all words, no action—meaning no touching. The final embrace had been cut altogether."[49]

Modern Iranian playwrights also face censorship. Beyond the requirements for modest clothing and the restrictions placed on interactions between males and females, the content of modern plays has also been affected. An online publication, the *Iranian*, says that "most plays published and staged in Persia must receive a seal of approval from the Islamic regime and in some way further its ideology."[50]

Occasionally, playwrights face severe penalties for opposing the government. One playwright, Soltanpuar, who had been active before the revolution, was executed in 1981 for so-called leftist activities. But most playwrights face less extreme consequences and are able to get their work produced as long as they cooperate with the government restrictions. According to the *Iranian*, "Playwrights working in Persia must consciously practice self-censorship and restrict their work in terms of the dress, actions, and appearance of their characters, in order to receive permission for performance."[51]

MUSIC

Like films and theater, music has also been suppressed by Iran's rigid enforcement of the government's interpretation of Islam. In the early 1980s, Iran's supreme leader Ayatollah Khomeini warned, "Western music dulls the mind because it involves pleasure and ecstasy, similar to drugs."[52] Khomeini banned all popular Persian music as well as Western music, from Mozart and Beethoven to Michael Jackson and Pink Floyd. According to author Robin Wright,

Of all the arts, music was a particularly sensitive issue in the Islamic republic. Iran's strict interpretation of Islam did not condone any influence that took a believer into

Two women practice playing traditional Iranian drums. Until recently, performance of most types of music was forbidden in Iran.

a state out of his or her being, whether by alcohol, drugs or music. As a result, the Iranian media featured little music in the early years besides military marches and the new national anthem.[53]

Traditional Persian poetry set to music was the only officially sanctioned form of music in Iran after the revolution. Some of these songs are very long, and it can take singers a lifetime to memorize the lyrics. The lyrics of most traditional music revolve around Islam, although some songs are about love and some about Persian victories over invading armies throughout history. The Iranian instruments used for accompaniment include the *tar*, a stringed instrument; the *dahol* and *zarb*, two sizes of drums; the *nay* and *sorna*, a flute and oboe; the *daryereh*, a tambourine; and the *demam*, a bagpipe. One popular singer, Shahram Nazeri, uses the poetry of Hafez, Sa'di, and other Persian poets but sets the lyrics to music that draws on traditional Iranian melodies played on modern instruments. Also incorporating modern rhythms and production techniques, the resulting music is distinctively Iranian but is popular with younger audiences.

Western music is still officially banned in Iran, but the ban has not stopped Iranians from listening to Western music and smuggling in contraband tapes, especially from nearby Turkey. According to the Lonely Planet guidebook, "Almost every taxi driver, especially in Tehran, seems to keep a cache of Turkish pop classics stashed under the dashboard."[54]

Most musicians featured on CDs that are available in Iran are men because women singers are taboo. One famous female singer and actress, Googoosh, was at one time immensely popular in Iran but was forbidden to perform after the Islamic Revolution in 1979. She did not perform for two decades, instead living quietly in a Tehran apartment with her husband. But in 2000, she was given permission by Iran's President Khatami to travel abroad to make a movie. She also gave her first concert in twenty-one years in Toronto, Canada, where she attracted a crowd of twelve thousand.

Iranian singer Googoosh performs in Toronto, Canada, in her first concert in twenty-one years.

And she released a new CD called *Zoroaster*, with songs sung in Farsi. The songs are about her life in Iran, especially what it was like not being allowed to perform. Googoosh says, "I don't think that any artist can face it, if you tell them they can't sing or can't act or can't live with your art for this long—for 20 years you can't work."[55]

Googoosh's popularity at home continues, and unauthorized copies of her CDs circulate in Iran even though they are officially banned. Circulating those CDs can be risky. People who are caught with an unauthorized CD might be ignored or merely warned by the authorities, or they might be arrested, fined, and even lashed, depending on where the offense occurs and on whether the government is tightening or loosening its control on public behavior.

Although Western-style rock and pop music are still officially banned in Iran, there are signs that the worst may be over for those who make music at home. According to one author, "Slowly but surely Iranian pop music is starting to re-emerge, albeit under the watchful eye of the Iranian authorities."[56] One popular singer, Muhammed Noori, who has been famous in Iran since before the revolution, performs songs with nationalistic lyrics. Even more suggestive of an easing of restrictions, Farhad, a clarinet player who was banned as a suspected Communist, is now allowed to perform in Iran again.

Still, being a musician in Iran today can be dangerous. A taxi driver and part-time musician in Tabriz named Azadi performs with a band at weddings and private parties. Because the music Azadi performs inspires people to dance—a taboo in Iran—he and his fellow band members have been arrested many times. Author Elaine Sciolino writes that police shot their guns into the air to break up a wedding reception where Azadi and his band were performing. Nevertheless, Azadi considers himself lucky because, "Unlike his fellow band members, he [has] never been lashed with a whip."[57]

The situation for all types of artists in Iran—caught between the desire to express themselves and the fear of being punished for it—illustrates the central challenge facing Iran: how to reconcile its devotion to Islam with the realities of modern life.

CHALLENGES TODAY AND TOMORROW

Iran faces an array of problems both within and beyond its own borders. To progress economically and as a member of the family of nations, it must find ways to resolve its conflicts with several of its neighbors. It must also improve relations with the wealthier and more technologically advanced nations of the West. Charges that elements of the Iranian government are involved in terrorism have dogged the country since the Islamic Revolution. Suspicions about Iran and its ties to terrorism were overshadowed by the attacks on the United States on September 11, 2001, by terrorists with no Iranian connection. Iranian officials expressed sympathy for the victims of the attacks and stressed their opposition to terrorism. Nevertheless, in the following weeks, Ayatollah Khamenei continued to refuse direct diplomatic contact with the United States, making it seem that Iran's international isolation might not lessen appreciably in the near future. Closer to home, Iran must find a way around the ongoing deadlock between the more liberal members of the legislative and executive branches and the conservative clerics who continue to hold key positions in the government.

A PRESIDENT WITH LIMITED POWER

The paralysis of the Iranian government results from conflict between the president and other elements of the government. Popularly elected president Muhammad Khatami has made many efforts to implement reforms in the Islamic Republic, such as increasing civil liberties and reducing restrictions on women and young people. But he faces opposition from conservative members of the government who do not want change. Conservative mullahs control the judiciary, intelligence, and state broadcasting network in Iran and therefore

93

DROUGHT IN IRAN

In 2001, after four consecutive years of drought, the Iranian government began water rationing in several provinces and cities throughout the country. The lives of some 25 million people have been affected by serious water shortages in eight of Iran's twenty-eight provinces. The book *Iran* by Pat Yale, Anthony Ham, and Paul Greenway states that in 2000, Iran's southern provinces suffered from the worst drought to hit the region in thirty years.

> More than half the population was left short of clean drinking water, and an estimated 800,000 sheep and cattle died of thirst or starvation. The waters of the Shahid Parsa Dam, which usually holds 11 million cubic meters [about 14 million cubic yards] of water, dried up, wildlife refuges were devastated, and lakes and lagoons shriveled; thousands of baby flamingoes were reported to have died after Lake Bakhtegan in southern Iran contracted from 50,000 hectares [about 125,000 acres] to a few muddy puddles. Pakistan announced that desperate crocodiles and wild boars had been spotted rampaging across its borders in search of water.

are in a position to block Khatami's reforms. According to the *Christian Science Monitor,*

> In Iran's bifurcated government, in which an elected president and parliament are in many ways subordinate to religious scholars charged with ensuring that laws and policies conform with Islam, Khatami's powers are limited.

> He has no control, for example, over the country's judges, who are empowered to act as investigators, prosecutors, and adjudicators.[58]

Conflict between the reformers and the conservatives can render the government impotent. For example, hard-line conservatives delayed Khatami's 2001 presidential inauguration by three days because of a dispute over appointments to a key government council. How Iran's political power struggles are resolved will determine how the country faces its many internal and external challenges.

One of the most difficult challenges faced by Iran is that it is perceived elsewhere in the world as inciting violence against its opponents. For example, in 1989 Iran's supreme leader, Khomeini, issued an official opinion, or fatwa, against Indian-born novelist Salman Rushdie. Rushdie is the author of *The Satanic Verses*, a novel many Muslims find offensive be-

Iranians protest the release of Salman Rushdie's The Satanic Verses.

cause of its portrayal of Muhammad and his family. As part of the fatwa, Ayatollah Khomeini called for Rushdie's execution for blasphemy. Rushdie, who was living in England, was forced to go into hiding, and the fatwa contributed a great deal to the souring of relations between Iran and the West. In 1998, President Khatami told a group of American reporters that the fatwa would not be enforced, saying, "We should consider the Salman Rushdie case as completely finished."[59] Despite Khatami's declaration, in 1999 more than half the members of the Majlis endorsed a statement that the fatwa was still in effect.

WOMEN IN IRANIAN SOCIETY

Other challenges Iran faces come as the result of conservative leaders' internal policies. The restrictions the conservative mullahs have placed on women have resulted in hardships for them and a lessening of the talent pool available to the country to get out of its economic and diplomatic messes. The challenge is to find ways to preserve the country's genuinely conservative Islamic values without losing access to the talents of over half the population.

President Khatami was reelected in June 2001 to a second four-year term, thanks largely to support from young people and women. However, Khatami's less restrictive policies regarding these two groups have fueled opposition by Iran's conservatives. For example, the deputy speaker of Iran's parliament, Mohsen Armin, complained that "it was not dignified for women to be put on display in government."[60]

The deputy speaker's comment created some controversy in Iran. In response to the comment, Jamileh Kadivar, a female member of Iran's parliament, made a public statement in favor of women in government positions. Kadivar told reporters at a press conference in Tehran, "We have repeatedly witnessed a violation of women's rights. . . . Certain key figures (in the government) still share dogmatic views dating back to 1,400 years." Kadivar, one of eleven female members of parliament, also said that men must change their views on women's competence, noting that President Khatami has supported women in management posts. "Despite the existing oppositions for the presence of women in various fields, Khatami elected two competent women to his cabinet."[61]

Iranian president Khatami, with the support of women and young people because of his less restrictive social policies, was reelected president in 2001.

Other prominent Iranian women point out that the conservatives' position on women's rights is not based in Islam. Mahboobeh Abbas-Gholizadeh is the editor of the Iranian magazine *Farzaneh* and a former student of Islamic law in Qom. She proposes that, because they cannot rely on help from the conservative clergy, Iranian women should develop new strategies to expand their legal rights. "What I say about women's rights is based on what I studied of religious law and logic. And I can tell you from knowing the Koran and *hadith* that whatever the clerics are doing is not what's written in the Koran. It's only their interpretation—their male and sometimes chauvinistic interpretation."[62]

The government is taking some steps to address problems experienced by women. In 2001, Iran had several shelters for abused women, and the government was planning a hotline for women who need help. Sahra Bonyanian, an outspoken proponent of women's rights in Iran, says that the hotline is in response to "increasing aggression against women at home . . . [due to] cultural and traditional role-models, prejudices, prejudgments." She says that as Iranian women become aware of the rights of women in Western countries, they are less likely to tolerate abuse at home. Bonyanian also says that Iranian women today "will no longer accept any aggression like their mothers used to."[63]

CRIMINAL JUSTICE

Iranian women have long been subject to harsh punishments if they break the law.

Iran's treatment of women tends to set the country apart from other developed nations in the world. Similarly, the ways in which Iran has sometimes applied Islamic law (Shariah), which seem to violate international standards for due process and human rights, have tended to isolate the nation. Iran's laws are harsh by Western standards. For example, according to one law based on the Shariah, adultery is

punishable by being stoned to death. A woman convicted of murder and adultery was stoned to death in July 2001 in Tehran's Evin prison. Amnesty International, a worldwide human rights monitoring group, says that at least seventy-five executions were carried out in Iran in 2000. Some executions were stonings, and some were public hangings.

Iran's government contends that its brand of justice has the backing of the people. In the southwestern city of Kouhdasht, a thirty-five-year-old woman was hanged in public in July 2001 for murdering a woman who discovered her plans to run away from home. According to Iran's state news agency, IRNA, the hanging took place before a large crowd, and "the people who gathered at the site of her execution were happy to see the murderer end up in the gallows."[64]

Even lesser crimes such as drinking alcohol, which is illegal under the Islamic regime, can bring harsh punishments such as flogging. Until recently, floggings were only rarely carried out in public. However, after Khatami's 2001 reelection there was a sharp increase in the number of public lashings. In July 2001, for example, fourteen young men between age eighteen and twenty-five were flogged publicly in Tehran before a crowd of onlookers. The men received between twenty and seventy lashes each as punishment for drinking alcohol and socializing with women who were not family members. The floggings took place at rush hour on a busy corner so that people going home from work would witness the punishment.

The public floggings were ordered by Khatami's hard-line opponents and defended by Iran's conservative judiciary chief, Ayatollah Mahmoud Hashemi Shahroudi. Reformers believe the floggings might have been designed to embarrass Khatami for his efforts to allow more freedom in Iran. The public floggings have been condemned by Khatami, who said in a speech to parliament, "In a society in which there is discrimination, poverty, and graft [illegal gain], you cannot expect youngsters not to break the law and stay [on] the right course. With tough punishments [alone], you cannot remove social corruption. . . . Social corruption has deep roots and to remove those roots we should work together." Khatami's conservative opponents vehemently defend their position. One hard-line cleric in Qom named Morteza Tehrani criticized reformers who challenged Islamic punishments, saying, "What

DISILLUSIONMENT IN IRAN

Many people in Iran have become disillusioned in recent years by their government, and supporters of Khatami have begun to complain that he is an ineffectual president because he has been unable to get reforms passed by his more moderate opponents. Khatami addressed these concerns in a speech he delivered to a group of students at Tehran University on December 22, 2001, explaining his views on moderation and how it affects the economy. His speech is quoted in "Excerpts of Khatami's Speech at Tehran University," available from the Iran Mania website (*www.iranmania.com*).

I fully believe that the people's disillusionment with the elected representatives will in no way mean that the people will once again vote for those to whom they have said "no" many times. Disappointing the people does not mean causing a rift between the people and the officials. It means destroying their hope in the [Islamic] system and pushing them towards outside of the [Islamic] system.

Moderation does not mean engaging in secret deals and compromise. This is not moderation, this is betraying the people. Moderation means striking a balance between the demands [and] potentials and prioritizing the demands in a situation where there are limitations on the resources. [Moderation means] efforts towards establishment of the modalities of living in the participatory society, democracy and the toleration of each other and the confronting moves that want to have a utilitarian approach to religion, freedom and independence of the nation.

Moderation means that we would accept the judgment of the majority, and simultaneously observe the rights of the minority. . . .

When the [economic] atmosphere is made insecure, when the problem-solving bills and plans are kept in suspension, and even the psychological security of managers and planners are threatened, the economic endeavors too will become difficult to undertake.

When an MP [member of parliament] is afraid of expressing his opinion lest he would be accused of attempting to overthrow [the Islamic order], when a manager is reluctant to work because he is afraid that he would be accused of plundering and thievery, the economic affairs of the nation will not be in order.

are these clownish words? You are destroying religion, challenging God's edicts. You think you can say anything just because you got the people's votes?"[65]

At least some ordinary Iranians are willing to speak out against this form of punishment. One woman complained, "Why are you whipping people's children like this on the streets?"[66] President Khatami and his supporters have said that public floggings are no longer appropriate punishments in Iran because they will further tarnish Iran's image abroad, making it more difficult for the nation to attract foreign investment and strengthen its economy.

FREEDOM OF EXPRESSION

Iran's clerics have stifled public debate over their policies, a move that has made the population fearful and harmed Iran's reputation, especially in the West. Iranians' right to free speech has been called into question in recent years, especially since Khatami's election in 1997, as many newspapers have been shut down by the government. According to Sciolino, "The conservative clerical establishment sees the new media outlets as the most subversive of its opponents."[67] One popular newspaper, *Jameah*, which began in February 1998, had a circulation of 300,000 a day. *Jameah*, which means "Society," printed articles that were critical of the government and the clergy. It was shut down in the summer of 1998, but its publisher and editor already had a license for another newspaper, which they opened a few days later under a new name, *Tous*. This newspaper was shut down after five weeks because it was seen as a threat to national security, and the publisher and editor were imprisoned. When they were released soon after, they reopened one newspaper after another under different names, each one being closed down by the government only to be followed by another newspaper with another name.

The conservatives' efforts to suppress speech may well be futile in the end. Muhammad Hadi Semati, a political scientist at Tehran University, explains,

> There are plenty of papers still out there. . . . One of them gets shut down and . . . two others pop up, so I think . . . that doesn't really change potentially the communication network that exists. There are at least 10, 15, other papers out there. And . . . quite a large number of

other channels; you know, Internet and the rest of the modern technology is definitely helpful.[68]

IRAN'S ECONOMY

Iranians are pushing the limits of freedom of expression, and many of Iran's people have been willing in recent years to say publicly that they are tired of poverty and want the government to do something about the economy. For many people, the challenge is simply to get enough to eat, get clothes to wear, and stay warm in the winter. For the government, the challenge is to deal with a broken economy and an increasingly angry public.

Iran is still under a trade embargo imposed by the United States in 1995 amid charges that Iran was supporting inter-

IRAN AND THE UNITED STATES

Iran's most recent conflict with a Western nation has been with the United States, which had great influence over internal politics in Iran during the second half of the twentieth century. From the early 1950s, the United States was in partial control of the Iranian oil industry and supplied substantial support to Iran's military and internal secret police. Many ordinary Iranians resented American influence in their country. More than twenty years after the Islamic Revolution, in which many Iranians attempted to rid the nation of foreign control and cultural influences, the conflict with the United States continues. Though there have been halting attempts to improve relations, in 2001 the two countries still had not reestablished diplomatic relations, and especially among more conservative clerics, America was blamed as the source of Iran's problems. For example, in August 2001, the Ayatollah Muhammad Emani-Kashani, a senior cleric, preached a sermon that was quoted in an article titled "Top Cleric Says U.S. Trying to Dishearten Youth from Islam" (available from the Islamic Republic News Agency at *www.irna.com*). In the sermon, the ayatollah said:

> The United States is plotting against the nation [Iran], the youth and the religion [Islam] to dishearten them. . . . The United States has waged an extensive propaganda [war] against the leadership (of Ayatollah Ali Khamenei) and the velayat-e faqih (the governance of supreme jurisprudent)

national terrorism. In addition, Iran's economy was devastated by the eight-year Iran-Iraq War and is still struggling to recover financially. According to *Washington Post* journalist John Anderson, Iranians want their government to provide more jobs and economic stability: "They've got horrendous unemployment. They've got very high inflation. They've got an amazing brain drain, with youths and some of the top technical people of the country and academics fleeing for jobs outside of Iran. . . . So the one thing that everybody is looking for is some kind of economic improvement here over the next four years."[69]

The economy is yet another area of reform in which Khatami faces opposition from conservatives. Khatami's government has tried to foster the country's economic

in a bid to play down the power of the two elements [of government] which can steer the country on the right path. . . . The enemy is aggravating economic, political and security tensions existing in the country and certain simple-minded stooges fuel the tensions in collusion with the enemies which would end in the disenchantment of the people with the leadership. . . . They (the enemies) are spreading corruption in the country to deprave the younger generation and take them away from religion.

Iranian demonstrators burn effigies and a U.S. flag in protest against American policies toward Iran.

development by implementing market reforms, such as privatization of industry, and by attracting foreign investment. But Khatami's attempts at economic reforms have been opposed by the conservatives, who say that foreign investment is unconstitutional and against Islamic law. Muhammad Hadi Semati thinks that it will require a great deal of dedication on Khatami's part to implement economic reform. According to Semati,

> [Khatami] understands that this is going to be a very long, drawn-out process, and he doesn't want to pick up the fight at every corner, at every crack that he runs into. But I think the democratization in Iran and political reform in Iran is a very, very bouncy road and I think for that he's saving himself and saving his energy and political capital. He has done great in terms of managing the reform process despite the pressure from below and opposition from . . . conservative elites.[70]

DRUG SMUGGLING AND DRUG ABUSE

The poor economy, unemployment, and lack of entertainment opportunities in the Islamic Republic have all contributed to the rampant social problems of drug smuggling and drug abuse—which represent yet another major challenge to the nation. Iran has spent millions of dollars in a crackdown on drugs and smuggling, but its military and police have captured only about 10 percent of the two thousand tons of drugs that have been estimated to pass through Iran every year.

In the first half of 2001, Iranian police forces arrested nearly fifteen hundred drug traffickers in the northeastern border region near Afghanistan. Yet the Iranian government complains that it is losing the increasingly violent battle. In the past two decades, more than three thousand Iranian militiamen, police, and army officers have died in encounters with drug traffickers.

In addition to smuggling, Iran faces the problem of drug use by its own citizens. The Iranian government's efforts to control drug addiction in Iran have not been entirely successful. Briongos explains that under the shah, though the penalty for drug trafficking was death, heroin addicts were

given the drug by the government to keep them from committing crimes to support their habits. But then there was a change:

Iranian troops reinforce the Iran-Afghan border in an effort to reduce drug trafficking.

With the Revolution, the death penalty for traffickers remained, but the supply to addicts was stopped. The new policy was to detoxify and rehabilitate the drug users; all those who wanted to take advantage of the new programme were asked to put their names down on the local register of people to be admitted to [the] hospital for treatment. The Islamic government has put a lot of effort into this strategy, but the problem hasn't gone away, nor is it really being solved. Without films or music, the people of [Iran] don't have anything to do if they go out, so they get together at home and kill time smoking opium over a charcoal burner, passing around the tulip-shaped pipe, to which they hold a glowing coal with a pair of tongs.[71]

THE PROSPECTS FOR REFORM

Azar Nafisi, an expert on Iranian politics, says that he thinks Iran's internal problems and the Iranian people's dissatisfaction with their government put President Khatami and his supporters in a nearly impossible situation. "Khatami's platform is a paradox; you cannot appease the extreme right and appease the people, the majority of whom want radical changes."[72]

The Iranian people successfully overthrew repressive governments twice in the twentieth century, only to see repression return in new forms. Many in the country are deeply dissatisfied with the interpretation of Islam adopted by the conservative clerics, especially Supreme Leader Ali Khamenei, and want President Khatami's government to push more forcefully for reform. Continuing to find ways to keep the battle a primarily political one rather than yet another armed conflict is perhaps the most important challenge facing Iran in the coming decades.

FACTS ABOUT IRAN

GEOGRAPHY

Area: 636,000 square miles; sovereignty claimed over territorial waters up to 12 nautical miles

Topography: A high central plateau surrounded by rugged mountains, deserts, and bodies of water. Mountain ranges include the Elburz in the north and the Zagros, which stretch from the northwest to the southeast. The highest peak is Mount Damavand at 18,934 feet; the lowest point is in the Caspian Sea approximately 89 feet below sea level.

Rivers: Karun and Karkheh in the west, Safid in the northwest, and Atrek on the northern border

Bordering countries: Turkey and Iraq on the west; Armenia, Azerbaijan, and Turkmenistan on the north; Afghanistan and Pakistan on the east

Major cities: Tehran, Esfahan, Mashhad, Rasht, Shiraz, Tabriz, and Qom

Climate: Variable; arid with scant annual precipitation except in the higher mountain peaks and the Caspian coastal plain

GOVERNMENT

Full name: Islamic Republic of Iran

Capital: Tehran

Government type: Islamic republic

President: Muhammad Khatami

Supreme leader: Ayatollah Sayyed Ali Khamenei

Political subdivisions: 28 provinces

PEOPLE

Population (2000): Approximately 66 million

Ethnic groups: Persian, 60 percent; Azeri, 25 percent; Kurd, 7 percent; Lors, 2 percent; Arab, Turkmen, Armenian, Assyrian, Baluchi, Georgian, Pashton, and others, 6 percent

Principal languages: Persian (Farsi; official), Azeri, Turkic, Kurdish, Arabic, and Lori

Religions: Shia Muslims, 89 percent; Sunni Muslims, 10 percent; Christians, Jews, Zoroastrians, Sikhs, Buddhists, and Baha'is, 1 percent

Education: Free; compulsory for ages 6–11

Literacy rate (2000): About 77 percent

Life expectancy (2000): Female, 71.69 years; male, 68.84

ECONOMY

Monetary unit: Rial

Exchange rate (Oct. 2000): 1,747.50 = $1 U.S.

Labor force: Services, 45 percent; mining, manufacturing, and construction, 31 percent; agriculture, 23 percent; other, 1 percent

Chief products: Oil, natural gas, iron, ore, copper, coal, wheat, cotton, rice, barley, fruits, sugar beets, caviar, manufacturing, textiles, carpets, food products, and cement

Gross domestic product per capita (2000): $5,000

NOTES

INTRODUCTION: A NATION OF CONTRASTS

1. Ana M. Briongos, *Black on Black: Iran Revisited.* Oakland, CA: Lonely Planet, 2000, pp. 10–11.

CHAPTER 1: THE LAND AND PEOPLE OF IRAN

2. Robin Wright, *The Last Great Revolution: Turmoil and Transformation in Iran.* New York: Vintage Books, 2001, p. xix.

3. Quoted in Jon Hemming, "Iran's Azeris Want More Cultural Recognition," Reuters News Service, June 3, 2001.

4. Christiane Bird, *Neither East nor West: One Woman's Journey Through the Islamic Republic of Iran.* New York: Pocket Books, 2001, p. 3.

5. Embassy of the Islamic Republic of Iran in Ottawa, "Geography." www.salamiran.org.

CHAPTER 2: FROM PERSIA TO THE ISLAMIC REPUBLIC

6. Sandra Mackey, *The Iranians: Persia, Islam, and the Soul of a Nation.* New York: Plume Books, 1996, p. 14.

7. Helen Chapin Metz, ed., *Iran: A Country Study.* Washington, DC: Library of Congress, 1989, p. 11.

8. Mackey, *The Iranians,* p. 39.

9. Mackey, *The Iranians,* p. 57.

10. Mackey, *The Iranians,* pp. 48–49.

11. Mackey, *The Iranians,* p. 6.

12. Mackey, *The Iranians,* p. 177.

13. Wright, *The Last Great Revolution,* p. 45.

14. Quoted in Wright, *The Last Great Revolution,* p. 45.

15. Wright, *The Last Great Revolution,* p. 15.

16. Wright, *The Last Great Revolution,* pp. xiii–xiv.

CHAPTER 3: RELIGION IN IRAN

17. Moojan Momen, *An Introduction to Shi'i Islam: The History and Doctrines of Twelver Shi'ism.* New Haven, CT: Yale University Press, 1985, p. 233.

18. Momen, *An Introduction to Shi'i Islam*, p. 235.

19. Momen, *An Introduction to Shi'i Islam*, p. 234.

20. Sachiko Murata and William C. Chittick, *The Vision of Islam.* St. Paul, MN: Paragon House, 1994, p. 13.

21. Murata and Chittick, *The Vision of Islam*, p. 12.

CHAPTER 4: DAILY LIFE IN THE ISLAMIC REPUBLIC

22. Mackey, *The Iranians*, p. 368.

23. Briongos, *Black on Black*, p. 113.

24. Mackey, *The Iranians*, p. 337.

25. Briongos, *Black on Black*, p. 67.

26. John Simpson and Tira Shubart, *Lifting the Veil: Life in Revolutionary Iran.* London: Hodder & Stoughton, 1995, pp. 217–218.

27. Quoted in Mackey, *The Iranians*, p. 13.

28. Briongos, *Black on Black*, p. 45.

29. Briongos, *Black on Black*, p. 27.

30. Roy Mottahedeh, *The Mantle of the Prophet: Religion and Politics in Iran.* Oxford, England: Oneworld Publications, 2000, pp. 26–27.

31. *Al-Quran*, rev. ed., Ahmed Ali, trans., Princeton, NJ: Princeton University Press, 1988, p. 304, Q24:58–59.

32. Quoted in Elaine Sciolino, *Persian Mirrors: The Elusive Face of Iran.* New York: Free Press, 2000, p. 101.

33. Wright, *The Last Great Revolution*, p. xix.

34. Briongos, *Black on Black*, p. 91.

35. Sciolino, *Persian Mirrors*, p. 35.

36. Briongos, *Black on Black*, p. 99.

37. "Illegal Cab Drivers and Garbage Collectors Fight for Living," *IranMania News*, December 7, 2001. www.iranmania.com.

38. Sciolino, *Persian Mirrors*, p. 147.

39. Sciolino, *Persian Mirrors,* p. 147.

40. Wright, *The Last Great Revolution,* p. 164.

41. Wright, *The Last Great Revolution,* p. 275.

CHAPTER 5: ART AND CULTURE

42. Quoted in "Iran's Contemporary Pottery and Ceramic Exhibition Opened in Tabriz," August 5, 2001. www.tehrantimes.com.

43. Jerome W. Clinton, trans., *The Tragedy of Sohrab and Rostam,* rev. ed. Seattle: University of Washington Press, 1996, p. xix.

44. Briongos, *Black on Black,* p. 61.

45. Peter Chelkowski and Hamid Dabashi, *Staging a Revolution: The Art of Persuasion in the Islamic Republic of Iran.* New York: New York University Press, 1999, p. 184.

46. Quoted in Wright, *The Last Great Revolution,* p. 127.

47. Sciolino, *Persian Mirrors,* p. 264.

48. Quoted in Wright, *The Last Great Revolution,* p. 78.

49. Wright, *The Last Great Revolution,* p. 78.

50. M.R. Ghanoonparvar, "Drama." www.iranian.com/Iranica.

51. Ghanoonparvar, "Drama."

52. Quoted in Wright, *The Last Great Revolution,* p. 86.

53. Wright, *The Last Great Revolution,* p. 86.

54. Pat Yale, Anthony Ham, and Paul Greenway, *Iran.* Oakland, CA: Lonely Planet, 2001, p. 43.

55. Quoted in Joanne Suh, "Iran's Pop Diva Googoosh Returns to the World Stage After Two Decades," October 9, 2000. www.cnn.com.

56. Yale, Ham, and Greenway, *Iran,* p. 44.

57. Sciolino, *Persian Mirrors,* p. 285.

CHAPTER 6: CHALLENGES TODAY AND TOMORROW

58. Cameron W. Barr, "In Iran, Repression Hits Home," *Christian Science Monitor,* June 20, 2001, p. 1.

59. Quoted in Sciolino, *Persian Mirrors,* p. 182.

60. Quoted in "Female MP Says Men's View on Women 1400

Years Old," *IranMania News,* July 2, 2001. www.iranmania. com.

61. Quoted in "Female MP Says Men's View on Women 1400 Years Old."

62. Quoted in Wright, *The Last Great Revolution*, p. 142.

63. Quoted in "Women Standing Up Against Physical, Mental Abuse at Home," *IranMania News,* July 3, 2001. www. iranmania.com.

64. Quoted in "Iran Hangs Female Murderer in Public," *Iran-Mania News,* July 5, 2001. www.iranmania.com.

65. Quoted in Michael Theodoulou, "Iran's Culture War Intensifies," *Christian Science Monitor,* August 21, 2001, p. 6.

66. Quoted in "Fourteen Youth Flogged in Public in Tehran Rush Hour," *IranMania News,* July 12, 2001. www. iranmania.com.

67. Sciolino, *Persian Mirrors,* p. 251.

68. Quoted in Scott Simon, "Mohammad Hadi Semati Discusses Economic Reform in Iran," National Public Radio, *Weekend Edition,* August 11, 2001. www.npr.org.

69. Quoted in "Power Struggle in Iran Delays Khatami's Inauguration," National Public Radio, *Morning Edition,* August 7, 2001. www.npr.org.

70. Quoted in Simon, "Mohammad Hadi Semati Discusses Economic Reform in Iran."

71. Briongos, *Black on Black,* pp. 40–41.

72. Quoted in "Jail Term Sparks Row in Iran Parliament," United Press International, August 21, 2001.

CHRONOLOGY

559–330 B.C.
The Achaemenian dynasty rules the Persian Empire.

312–190 B.C.
Alexander the Great and his successors, the Seleucid dynasty, rule Persia.

190 B.C.–A.D. 224
The Parthian dynasty rules Persia.

224–637
The Sassanian dynasty rules Persia; Zoroastrianism is the official religion.

642
Arab Muslims defeat the Sassanian army at Nahavand, completing the Islamic conquest of Persia.

1051–1220
Seljuq Turks gain control of Persia.

1220–1380
Mongol tribes invade Persia, destroying cities and massacring inhabitants.

1501–1722
The Safavid dynasty rules Persia, declaring Shia Islam the state religion.

1794–1925
The Qajar dynasty rules Persia.

1906–1911
The Constitutional Revolution leads to a new constitution limiting royal power.

1921
Persian Cossack Brigade officer Reza Khan leads a coup against the government.

1925

The Qajar dynasty is officially deposed; Reza Khan becomes Reza Shah Pahlavi.

1935

The shah changes the country's name to Iran.

1941

Reza Shah Pahlavi abdicates in favor of his son, Muhammad Reza Shah Pahlavi.

1944

Reza Shah Pahlavi dies.

1961

The shah dissolves the Majlis.

1979

In January, the shah flees Iran amid growing opposition; in February, the Ayatollah Khomeini returns from exile; in April, Iranians vote to establish the Islamic Republic of Iran; in October, the physically ailing shah is allowed to enter the United States.

1979–1981

The hostage crisis begins on November 4, 1979, when Iranian students seize the U.S. embassy in Tehran and hold more than fifty U.S. citizens hostage for 444 days.

1980–1988

The Iran-Iraq War devastates Iran's economy, destroys several towns and hundreds of villages, and claims the lives of up to 500,000 Iranians.

1989

Ayatollah Khomeini dies in June and is succeeded as *faqih* by Ayatollah Ali Khamenei; Ali Akbar Hashemi Rafsanjani is elected president.

1997

Muhammad Khatami is elected president.

2001

Khatami is reelected president.

FOR FURTHER READING

Farid ud-Din Attar, *The Conference of the Birds*. New York: Penguin Books, 1984. One of the most important classical Persian poems, *The Conference of the Birds* is an allegory of the mystical life.

Peter Avery and John Heath Stubbs, trans., *The Ruba'iyat of Omar Khayyam*. New York: Penguin Books, 1979. One of the first known and most frequently translated Persian poems in the West.

Coleman Barks and John Moyne, trans., *The Essential Rumi*. San Francisco: HarperCollins, 1995. Rumi, who was born in what is now Afghanistan, has been one of the most beloved poets in Iran for many centuries.

Jerome W. Clinton, trans., *The Tragedy of Sohrab and Rostam*. Rev. ed. Seattle: University of Washington Press, 1996. This is a recent translation of an important section of the vast Persian epic *Shaname*.

Editors of Time-Life Books, *Persians: Masters of Empire*. Alexandria, VA: Time-Life Books, 1995. This book gives the early history of Iran and includes several remarkable photographs of ancient buildings and ruins.

Manucher Farmanfarmaian and Roxane Farmanfarmaian, *Blood and Oil: Inside the Shah's Iran*. New York: Modern Library, 1997. This is the inside story of Iran's battle to develop its oil industry during the twentieth century.

Martin Forward, *Muhammad: A Short Biography*. Oxford, England: Oneworld Publications, 1997. An accessible biography of the Prophet of Islam.

Cyrus Ghani, *Iran and the Rise of Reza Shah: From Qajar Collapse to Pahlavi Rule*. London: I.B. Tauris, 1998. Examines the life and political career of the first Pahlavi shah.

Dilip Hiro, *The Longest War: The Iran-Iraq Military Conflict.* New York: Routledge, 1991. One of the standard histories of the war.

Jennifer A. Hurley, ed., *Islam: Opposing Viewpoints.* San Diego: Greenhaven Press, 2001. This book presents articles that debate some of the issues facing Islam today.

Moojan Momen, *A Short Introduction to the Baha'i Faith.* Oxford, England: Oneworld Publications, 1997. An overview of the practice of the Baha'i Faith today, with a brief summary of its history.

Gary Sick, *All Fall Down: America's Tragic Encounter with Iran.* New York: Penguin Books, 1986. This book focuses on the Iran hostage crisis of 1979 to 1981.

WORKS CONSULTED

BOOKS

Abol Hassan Bani-Sadr, *My Turn to Speak: Iran, the Revolution and Secret Deals with the U.S.* Washington, DC: Brassey's (U.S.), 1991. The Islamic Republic's first elected president details his side of the story of the revolution, his time in office, and the reasons for his exile.

Christiane Bird, *Neither East nor West: One Woman's Journey Through the Islamic Republic of Iran.* New York: Pocket Books, 2001. This book is by a writer who lived in Iran for several years during her childhood and then traveled alone through the Islamic Republic in the late 1990s.

Ana M. Briongos, *Black on Black: Iran Revisited.* Oakland, CA: Lonely Planet, 2000. The author gives a glimpse of what life in Iran was like when she was first a student there in the 1970s and during an extended visit in the mid-1990s.

Daniel Brumberg, *Reinventing Khomeini: The Struggle for Reform in Iran.* Chicago: University of Chicago Press, 2001. A scholarly look at the politics of Iran since Khomeini's death in 1989.

Peter Chelkowski and Hamid Dabashi, *Staging a Revolution: The Art of Persuasion in the Islamic Republic of Iran.* New York: New York University Press, 1999. The authors provide a history of cinema in Iran and look at how the revolutionary government used propaganda to further the ideals of the revolution.

Erika Friedl, *Women of Deh Koh: Lives in an Iranian Village.* New York: Penguin Books, 1991. This book examines the issues confronting women in the Islamic Republic of Iran.

Ruhollah Khomeini, *Islam and Revolution: Writings and Declarations of Imam Khomeini, 1941–1980.* Berkeley, CA: Mizan Press, 1981. An extensive collection of Khomeini's

writings, mainly from the decade preceding the revolution.

Sandra Mackey, *The Iranians: Persia, Islam, and the Soul of a
Nation*. New York: Plume Books, 1996. Examines the effects of Iran's Persian and Islamic heritages on politics and
daily life.

Helen Chapin Metz, ed., *Iran: A Country Study*. Washington,
DC: Library of Congress, 1989. Although somewhat dated,
this book is still an excellent source for information on the
history and geography of Iran.

Baqer Moin, *Khomeini: Life of the Ayatollah*. New York: St.
Martin's Press, 1999. This biography covers the life of Iran's
first supreme leader, focusing on his role in organizing the
revolution and putting his ideas on Islamic government
into practice.

Moojan Momen, *An Introduction to Shi'i Islam: The History
and Doctrines of Twelver Shi'ism*. New Haven, CT: Yale
University Press, 1985. A detailed look at Shia Islam, especially as it is practiced in Iran.

Roy Mottahedeh, *The Mantle of the Prophet: Religion and
Politics in Iran*. Oxford, England: Oneworld Publications,
2000. This account of modern Iran is drawn from the stories of participants in the country's political and cultural
life before, during, and after the revolution.

Sachiko Murata and William C. Chittick, *The Vision of Islam*.
St. Paul, MN: Paragon House, 1994. A detailed and illumi-
nating account of the theology and practice of Islam.

Maria O'Shea, *Iran: A Guide to Customs and Etiquette*. Port-
land, OR: Graphic Arts Center, 1999. This book offers in-
sight on culture and society in Iran.

Taj al-Saltana, *Crowning Anguish: Memoirs of a Persian
Princess from the Harem to Modernity, 1884–1914*. Washington, DC: Mage Publishers, 1993. The story of the
daughter of a Qajar ruler of Iran.

Elaine Sciolino, *Persian Mirrors: The Elusive Face of Iran*.
New York: Free Press, 2000. An in-depth look at conditions
in postrevolutionary Iran.

John Simpson and Tira Shubart, *Lifting the Veil: Life in Revolutionary Iran.* London: Hodder & Stoughton, 1995. An account of life in Iran in the early 1990s, by two British journalists.

Alison Wearing, *Honeymoon in Purdah: An Iranian Journey.* New York: Picador USA, 2000. A young Canadian writer tells the often funny story of her extended visit to the Islamic Republic.

Robin Wright, *The Last Great Revolution: Turmoil and Transformation in Iran.* New York: Vintage Books, 2001. The author, an American journalist, examines the multitude of changes in Iran during the first two decades after the revolution.

Pat Yale, Anthony Ham, and Paul Greenway, *Iran.* Oakland, CA: Lonely Planet, 2001. This guidebook offers information on topics such as the history, architecture, society, customs, and culture of Iran.

PERIODICALS

Cameron W. Barr, "In Iran, Repression Hits Home," *Christian Science Monitor*, June 20, 2001.

Jon Hemming, "Iran's Azeris Want More Cultural Recognition," Reuters News Service, June 3, 2001.

"Jail Term Sparks Row in Iran Parliament," United Press International, August 21, 2001.

Michael Theodoulou, "Iran's Culture War Intensifies," *Christian Science Monitor*, August 21, 2001.

INTERNET SOURCES

Embassy of the Islamic Republic of Iran in Ottawa, "Geography," www.salamiran.org.

"Female MP Says Men's View on Women 1400 Years Old," *IranMania News*, July 2, 2001. www.iranmania.com.

"Fourteen Youth Flogged in Public in Tehran Rush Hour," *IranMania News*, July 12, 2001. www.iranmania.com.

M.R. Ghanoonparvar, "Drama." www.iranian.com/Iranica.

"Illegal Cab Drivers and Garbage Collectors Fight for Living," *IranMania News*, December 7, 2001. www.iranmania.com.

"Iran's Contemporary Pottery and Ceramic Exhibition Opened in Tabriz," August 5, 2001. www.tehrantimes.com.

"Iran Hangs Female Murderer in Public," *IranMania News*, July 5, 2001. www.iranmania.com.

Fen Montaigne, "Iran: Testing the Waters of Reform," *National Geographic*, July 1999. www.nationalgeographic.com.

"Power Struggle in Iran Delays Khatami's Inauguration," National Public Radio, *Morning Edition*, August 7, 2001. www.npr.org.

Scott Simon, "Mohammad Hadi Semati Discusses Economic Reform in Iran," National Public Radio, *Weekend Edition*, August 11, 2001. www.npr.org.

Joanne Suh, "Iran's Pop Diva Googoosh Returns to the World Stage After Two Decades," October 9, 2000. www.cnn.com.

"Top Cleric Says U.S. Trying to Dishearten Youth from Islam," Islamic Republic News Agency, August 17, 2001. www.irna.com.

"Women Standing Up Against Physical, Mental Abuse at Home," *IranMania News*, July 3, 2001. www.iranmania.com.

WEBSITES

Iranian Cultural and Information Center (www.persia.org). This site provides information on the culture and history of Iran.

Iranica (www.iranian.com/Iranica). This online publication gives information on a variety of topics about Iran.

Iran Mania (www.iranmania.com). This website contains links to useful information on a variety of topics, including Iran's history, religion, government, and culture.

Islamic Republic News Agency (www.irna.com). This website provides links to news articles and current affairs in Iran.

Salam Iran (www.salamiran.org). This website provides information on topics such as music, geography, economy, and current events in Iran.

INDEX

PICTURE CREDITS

About the Author

Cherese Cartlidge is a freelance writer and editor. Ms. Cartlidge attended New Mexico State University, where she received a B.A. in psychology, and is currently a graduate student at the University of Georgia. She and her two children, Olivia and Tommy, have lived in Georgia since 1997.